True Crime
in Titletown, U.S.A.

Cold Cases

Tracy C. Ertl and Mike R. Knetzger

Badger Books Inc.
Oregon, Wis.

Published by Badger Books Inc.
Edited by Mary Lou Santovec
Cover design by George McCue
Cover photo courtesy of the Green Bay Police Department
Printed in the U.S.A.

ISBN+10 1-932542-17-5
ISBN+13 978-1-932542-17-2

Badger Books Inc./Waubesa Press
P.O. Box 192
Oregon, WI 53575
Toll-free phone: (800) 928-2372
Fax: (800) 928-2372
Email: books@badgerbooks.com
Web site: www.badgerbooks.com

CONTENTS

Dedication 5

Introduction 7

Cannard Extortion Case 13

The Golden Pheasant 59

South Side State Bank Robbery 97

Epilogue 190

About the authors 191

Bibliography 193

Index 195

DEDICATION

John (Jack) Van Veghel and Lucille Birdsall were stolen from their families too early and too brutally. This book is dedicated in part to their families, past and present. A cold case is only a cold case until there is an un-chased lead. It is our desire that this case, and others described in our book, go from cold to warm.

Heart felt thanks to Norb and Mary Van Beckum and John and Diane Van Veghel. As a journalist at heart but a working police/fire dispatcher, this book would not have been possible without the support of my husband, Terry; my three children, Andrew, Christine & Bradley; and the belief of the rest of my family, friends and coworkers at Brown County Public Safety Communications. Finally, thank you to all teachers, classroom and otherwise, who have developed my inquisitive nature, including former Brown County Sheriff Tom Hinz and former *Green Bay Press-Gazette* Metro Editor Michael Blecha. Hinz told me I could do anything. Blecha told me never to lose my enthusiasm. Yes sir(s)!

Also, feelings of honor in having interviewed my first centurian, 102-year-old Julia Dorothy (Altman) Slupinski of Green Bay, and to her family for bringing her to us. As the widow of South Side Bank teller Frank Slupinski, Mrs. Slupinski showed incredible courage and clarity in recalling the events surrounding her husband's survival of the robbery.

— Tracy C. Ertl
July 2005

This book is dedicated to the families of Detective August Delloye, twice shot in the line of duty and Chief Thomas E.

Hawley, who served as Police Chief for Titletown, USA for 49 years.

    This book would not have been possible without the loving patience and support of my wonderful wife, Lisa and our three children, Ashley, Madeline & Noah. I thank my loving parents who, many years ago, forced me to see an English tutor and provide me with the prerequisite skills to write this work. Finally, thank you to Deb Anderson at the University of Wisconsin-Local History Research Center, the staff of the Brown County Library — Local History Center, my good friend and colleague Jeremy Muraski for his technical assistance, and all the willing accomplices who agreed to submit to countless hours of interviews — you know who you are.

— Michael R. Knetzger
July 2005

INTRODUCTION

A few years ago, while peering through the glass display cases on the second floor of the Green Bay Police Department, a little known history book peered back. The book, written in 1995 by members of the police department, chronicled, among other things, two unsolved crimes: the Cannard extortion case (1928) and the South Side State Bank robbery (1931). Each story was briefly summarized, leaving the reader longing for more and wondering why these fascinating cases were never solved. This is where the journey began.

True Crime in Titletown, U.S.A. — Cold Cases takes you back to the days of Prohibition, where rumrunners and bank robbers reigned. The names of Capone, Dillinger, Machine Gun Kelly, Baby Face Nelson and Polack Joe Saltis were among the most popular. The cities of Chicago and St. Paul were their homes, but many of them preferred Wisconsin as their vacation destination to get away from business and authorities alike. They shed their Tommy guns for swimsuits and didn't plan anything that would bring them unneeded attention.

"Machine Gun Thugs Battle Police, Get Away in Fast Auto"
— Green Bay Press-Gazette, July 20, 1931

A series of .45-caliber Tommy gun rounds cut through the squad car like butter wounding three officers, one seriously. They had interrupted a bank robbery in progress and mistakenly parked in front of the gangster's vehicle. The streets erupted in gunfire while the bandits made their escape, never to be seen again. "Dillinger, it had to have been Dillinger," was the thought for decades. Indeed, he fit the profile. The case faded into history, a cold case in its truest sense. Nobody ever took a serious look at it, until now!

"Police After Blackmailers, Stage Battle…" — Green Bay *Press-Gazette, January 10, 1928*

Police officers are given the legal responsibility to justifiably take the life of another, and that person is normally a criminal. That was not the case in 1928 when a detective and officers engaged in a tragic gun battle with each other. Who were these Triangle Club blackmailers and how did police mistakenly target each other?

We ran with thesetwo stories and when word got out, we were made aware of a third, shocking, unsolved crime known to locals as the Golden Pheasant Murders. On Monday, May 19, 1930, the owner of the Golden Pheasant Roadhouse and his waitress were hacked to death in their sleep. He never woke up and died where he lay, with the covers still tucked underneath his chin. She, on the other hand, woke up during the assault and made a valiant but feeble attempt to protect herself from the hatchet-wielding attacker. She, too, met her demise. The killer fled, leaving a trail of evidence behind, never to be seen again. "Most Gruesome…" hardly described the blood-painted scene that was discovered by a young boy sent by his mother to check on the victims. What he saw shocked not only Green Bay, but the entire state.

Investigating a typical cold case is a challenging task. Though the leads have dried up, much of the physical evidence, potential suspects and witnesses are usually still around. However, taking on a historic cold case, where all leads, victims, witnesses, suspects and evidence are gone, is another matter. Both of them are in a league of their own. Our three cases played in that "historic cold case" division.

Early on it was discovered that all of the police and investigative reports were gone. The physical evidence — destroyed. The police officers, detectives, victims and potential suspects — deceased. Forced, we focused our efforts on what few resources were still available, the most extensive being newspaper articles preserved on microfilm. It's no secret to the experienced student or researcher, that searching through microfilm is a tedious process. Countless hours were spent scrolling through microfiche looking for leads; the names of victims and witnesses, descriptions of physical evidence, methods of operation and much more. Then, through pure luck, a gold mine of original resources was found, tucked away in a large closet in the basement of the police department. In 1929, little did the first female police patron, Ida Graves, and those that followed her realize how much they helped us gather materials for this work by simply cutting out crime-related newspaper articles and pasting them in a scrapbook. Yellowed and aged, these articles not only saved us significant time and energy, they generated valuable leads.

However, we still needed somebody who was there, over 70 years ago, to help recreate these events and take us beyond the newspaper headlines. Tenacity, motivation, luck — they all played a role in finding eyewitnesses, family members and police officers who worked alongside the embattled veterans. Some remained in Wisconsin and others were located across the country. We sought them out and they helped make these cold cases warm again.

Written in a narrative non-fiction fashion, *True Crime in Titletown, U.S.A. — Cold Cases* takes you back to the scene of the crime. Riveting descriptive narrative will help you re-live the shootouts, murder, mayhem, the investigations and their aftermath. You will feel the impact that these crimes had on the police officers, their families and the citizens of the community.

The passage of time and lack of first person sources required the use of poetic license to give these stories a dramatic flare. In many cases we will never know exactly what the charaters said. However, our extensive research, professional criminal justice and crime reporting backgrounds and investigative insight allowed us to recreate narrative that was probably spoken at the time of these events.

If anybody has any information about these cases or others that should be written about, please visit our Web site at www.truetitletowncrime.com and contact us by clicking on the "Tips" link.

Now, sit back and enjoy the journey into *True Crime in Titletown, U.S.A. — Cold Cases.*

— Tracy Ertl and Mike Knetzger
July 2005
Green Bay, Wis.

True Crime
in Titletown, U.S.A.
Cold Cases

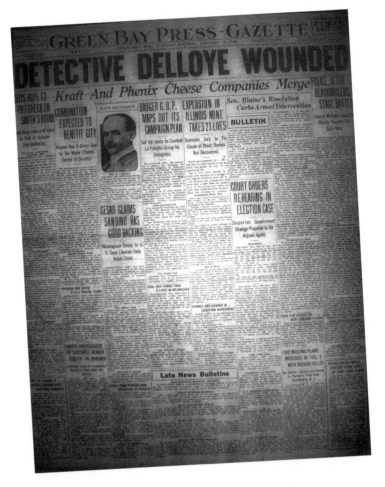

"Detective Delloye Wounded" — Green Bay Press-Gazette, Jan. 10, 1928.

CANNARD EXTORTION CASE

Saturday, December 24, 1928 — 136 S. Roosevelt Street

Christmas Eve, a time to spread good news and cheer and reflect on all the blessings received throughout the year. It would be anything but that on this particular day. Saturday, December 24, 1928, marked the beginning of a unique chain of events that would put a police detective in the hospital, leaving him nearly unrecognizable. He was suffering from over 175 rounds of buckshot scattered throughout his body from a gun battle with fellow officers. Not only was this a case of mistaken identity on the part of the police, but the extortionists as well.

Like dry, cold bones chilled from the midday winter air, the hinges creaked as the front door of 136 S. Roosevelt Street closed slowly behind its rightful owner. With his newspaper and mail in hand, Mr. William H. Cannard sat down in the front room of his modest two-story house, which sat mid-block along this quiet residential street. Tree-lined sidewalks and snow-covered lawns highlighted the house and other middle-class homes around it. Only a hundred feet south of E. Walnut Street, the city's main east side road, it was a perfect location for families with school-aged kids and dedicated Packer fans alike. East High School and the original City Stadium, home of the Green Bay Packers from 1925-1956, were only two blocks east.

Cannard placed the few envelopes and last minute Christmas cards aside on the end table while he perused the headlines of the day. "Couple Asphyxiated in Auto at Kelly

Lake" and "Grayson Airplane Missing" appeared in large black print. Hoping to become a woman pioneer and fly across the Atlantic, Mrs. Frances W. Grayson, against the advice of weathermen, took off from Roosevelt Field, New York in an amphibian plane headed for Newfoundland. Her plane never arrived and was feared lost somewhere near Cape Cod. Equally sad, two families had lost their children, a son and daughter, after they accidentally poisoned themselves while sitting inside an idling coupe near Kelly Lake. A Christmas "gift" that nobody would want to open. On the lighter side, Cannard chuckled when he read, "Green Bay is 'All Set' for Santa Claus' Visit Tonight." He looked at his decorated fireplace mantel and remembered those times when his now-grown kids, sixteen-year-old Richard and eighteen-year-old Anice, would awake very early in the morning on Christmas day and anxiously wait to tear open their presents. His kids still loved Christmas, but for different reasons.

Turning his attention to the unopened envelopes, Cannard moved his metal mail opener along the top seams, being careful not to damage the contents. A Christmas card or even some holiday greetings from business associates brought upon a warm smile or slight chuckle. However, one particular envelope drew his attention. A standard size letter envelope, handwritten and addressed to Cannard, didn't contain a return address. Figuring the sender may have forgotten to place it in the upper left corner, he opened it, not thinking twice. He unfolded it and began to read the typewritten text to himself.

Mr. Cannard,

This is not a joke! In the next seven days, New Years Eve, you will deliver a sum of $1,000 to a location east of the city off of Highway 78. It will be marked with a wooden box, placed on top of a fence post, which will have three white lights forming a triangle, with a red light in the center. Place the money inside the *box by 9:00 p.m. Failure to follow these instructions will result in you being shot. Don't get the police involved.*

The Triangle Club

In disbelief, Cannard read through the note a couple times and attempted to remain calm to avoid alarming his family, especially his wife, Marie. "Why me?" he wondered to himself. "There are lots more men in town with more money than me."

Why would they target this middle-aged family man and superintendent of the Bay West Paper Company? His most significant accomplishment to date was a patent awarded to him for the development of a machine that put wrappers around rolls of toilet paper. An accomplishment, yes, but it didn't earn him riches or fame. He was an average, middle-class wage earner with little or no notoriety. He wasn't a rumrunner and didn't hang out in houses of ill repute where the writers of such a letter may be found. It was a mystery and he hoped it would stay that way.

Cannard folded the note and tucked it away in his pants' pocket. A few hours later, after saying good night to Richard and Anice, he broke the news to his wife.

"Honey," Cannard began, clearing his throat and speaking slowly, while holding the letter in his right hand. "We received this letter today. Please do your best to stay calm and not upset the children."

He handed it to her and she slowly unfolded and read it. Her eyes widened while she covered her mouth and gulped in disbelief. Obviously shaken, Cannard went on, "I think we just need to ignore it. Keep things calm around here."

Marie disagreed and argued, "Are you kidding? William, we must take this to the police! What about you? Me? Our kids? We can't risk our family!"

Cannard did his best to calm her, "Honey, think about it. Why would they focus on us? What do we really have to offer? This could just be some sick joke. Lets sit on it a few days and if anything else strange begins to happen, we will take it directly to the police, I promise."

Marie was hesitant but agreed to follow her husband's wishes. Cannard folded up the letter and placed it in a desk drawer. Wanting never to see it again, they both walked up to bed, still hoping to enjoy Christmas Day. Maybe it was just a bad dream and a good night's rest would make it all go away.

Christmas Day came and went. Each day closer to New Year's Eve imparted more and more stress upon the Cannards. They masked it well, keeping it inside, and never told their kids about it. Right up to the very moment of the scheduled "drop" time, no other letters arrived, no strange phone calls, no strange vehicles, and no strange people were seen around the house.

New Year's Day arrived and Cannard reassured Marie that everything was going to be okay. Convinced and believing it to be a sick joke, he relaxed a bit. However, many "What if" questions still lingered in his mind. "What if it were real?" "What if I walked out of the house to go to work and was shot?" "What if my family had to continue living without me?" Cannard did his best to push these thoughts aside and prepared for the work week ahead.

Monday, January 2, 1928

Up early in the morning and off to work for his 8:00 am start time, Cannard didn't change his routine. He drove his same vehicle, a mid-1920's black Hudson, took the same route and parked in the same place. Though he did become more vigilant, paying attention to his surroundings and making sure he wasn't being followed or watched. He returned home each night, again taking the same route and grabbing his mail and newspaper on the way inside to greet his family for dinner. Before sitting down, out of view from his kids, he nervously thumbed through the mail, hoping to never receive another letter threatening his life.

Tuesday, Wednesday, Thursday, Friday... each passing day made it a bit easier. No other demands were received. Convinced it was a simple case of mistaken identity, the Cannards looked forward to a well-deserved and "normal" relaxing weekend.

Saturday, January 7, 1928 — afternoon

"Oh no, not again!" Cannard thought to himself while holding another envelope addressed to him in the same writing as the first extortion letter. His attempts to convince himself otherwise were quickly halted when, with shaking hands, he opened, unfolded and silently read the typewritten note:

Mr. Cannard,

It is a shame that you didn't comply with our first demand. We will give you one more chance before killing you. This time, you have only a few days to comply. The amount, $1,000, has not changed and neither has the location. By Monday, January 9 at 9:00 p.m place the money in the lighted wooden box on top of a post east of here off Hwy 78. No police, no problems.

The Triangle Club

Cannard immediately took it to Marie and before she could even speak, he prepared himself to leave for the police department. Marie insisted that they tell the kids. Cannard agreed, but wanted to first meet with police and determine the best course of action. He walked to his desk, obtained the first letter and kissed his wife goodbye.

Tearing her apart, Marie kept it all inside while she watched her husband back the Hudson out of the driveway, drive north on S. Roosevelt, then west on E. Walnut Street towards downtown.

Cannard rolled up to City Hall, 122 N. Jefferson St., and parked on the street, right in front of the main entrance. He traversed the gray concrete steps, walked through the heavy wooden doors and a quick right turn led him into the Green Bay Police Department.

He was greeted by a front desk officer. Obviously shaken and nervous, the front desk officer took note of Cannard's nervous condition and offered assistance. Cannard unfolded both extortion letters and placed them on the desk for the officer to read. The typewritten words spoke for themselves and the officer asked Cannard to excuse him for a moment while he walked back to the detective bureau. A few minutes later, Cannard was introduced to Detective August "Gus" Delloye and they walked back into the division together.

Det. Delloye offered him a seat, which he gladly accepted. Delloye, seated behind his desk, carefully handled the letters by the edges and laid them out in front of him. He slowly read through each one, line-by-line. A tough beat cop of eleven years turned detective, Delloye was a stickler for details. He meticulously noted the similarities. Typewritten in the same style and font. Same demands. Same drop location. Same signature. It was obvious that they came from the same person(s). Besides the Triangle Club food distributors in the Upper Peninsula, Delloye had never heard of such a group.

"When did you receive the first letter?" Det. Delloye inquired. Cannard explained that the first one had been received on Christmas Eve and thinking it was a joke, he filed it away. "But the second letter I received today. And we are scared to death. We need your assistance," Cannard pleaded. Delloye assured him that the police department would do all they could to help apprehend these blackmailers.

Delloye realized that he couldn't do this alone and phoned his friend, partner and boss, Lieutenant Martin Burke. Delloye filled him in and he agreed to come over to the station at once. While waiting for Burke to arrive, Delloye gathered additional information about Cannard's family.

"What's the motive? Why would they focus on you and your family?" Delloye asked.

Cannard had the same question. Then it dawned on him. Nearly shouting, "My brother, Arthur, Arthur Cannard. He's the cashier of the Farmer's Exchange Bank…"

Delloye interrupted him, "And they confused you with him?"

"Yes, exactly." replied Cannard.

Delloye handed Cannard the phone to call his brother. For the first time, Cannard told Arthur about the threatening letter and passed the receiver to Delloye. "Have you received any similar letters? Have you had any dealings with people who might have a grudge against you? Have you received any strange phone calls? Have you seen any strange people at the bank? Do you have any idea who might be threatening your brother, William?" Arthur answered no to all of these questions and was unable to supply any leads. Delloye encouraged him to call if he became aware of anything, however so slight, related to the investigation. Delloye gave the phone back to Cannard who ended the conversation, saying goodbye possibly for the last time.

Delloye continued his preliminary investigation and obtained the names of Cannard's wife and kids, their daily routines, the type of vehicle they drove, where they worked, where they went to school, who they were friends with, where they socialized and with whom they had shared the extortion attempt. The information would help them formulate a plan to apprehend the "Triangle Club" members or, at the very least, supply a lead to follow up. Question after question was met with a dead end. There wasn't much to go on. The only possible way to apprehend them would be a well-planned "drop."

The twenty-nine year veteran, Lt. Burke, arrived and

Delloye shared all of the information with him. Known as a walking records department, Burke reached into his vest pockets and pulled out stacks of index cards. Each card contained the names of known criminals, their histories and methods of operation (M.O.). Although a long shot, Burke shared some of the more likely names with Cannard and he didn't recognize any of them. None of their M.O.s matched.

Burke agreed, a "drop" at the appointed time would provide an opportunity to make an arrest. However, they didn't know the exact location of the lighted wooden box. Delloye and Burke considered staking out the area of Hwy. 78, but realized they might have to drive all the way to Sturgeon Bay before finding it. They scrapped this idea and came up with their final plan.

In consultation with Cannard, it was decided to have him drive his Hudson with Delloye and Burke hidden in the back seat. Cannard would drive east on Hwy. 78 until he found the lighted wooden box. When he found it, Cannard was to place the "drop," a brown paper bag stuffed with newspaper made to look like a sack of money, inside the box and then drive on. Delloye would then get out a couple hundred feet down the road, walk toward the drop point, conceal himself and wait for the "Triangle Club" to arrive and claim their prize. To prevent anything from happening to Cannard, Burke would wait inside the Hudson with him and, if needed, also assist in the apprehension. They reviewed and refined the plan a few times until each one was clear of their roles.

Then they turned their attention to the safety of Cannard's family. Burke offered to assign an officer to the Cannard house for the next couple of days. For now, Cannard declined the offer. Delloye insisted, at the very least, that an extra foot patrol be assigned to the area. Burke agreed and Cannard was thankful, preferring this low-key approach.

Cannard had yet to break the news to his kids and wondered if he should tell them and, if so, how? Burke and Delloye suggested that he should be straightforward with them. It was too risky not to. Everybody in the house needed to be more alert, vigilant and prepared for the unthinkable.

Delloye kept the letters as evidence and Cannard thanked them for their assistance. Random thoughts poured through Cannard's mind making the half-mile drive home seem to last forever.

Could my life end in the next 48 hours? Maybe I should let a police officer stay at the house? How are my kids going to take this? What if they are lurking around or inside the house now?

Questions turned to rage and he screamed inside: *Who the hell would do this to me?*

Cannard sat everybody down in the front room and broke the news. Just as directed, he was straightforward. He revealed all the details and encouraged them not to worry. Anice, seeing the obvious stress and concern on her mother's face, was shaken up a bit. Richard, on the other hand, found this to be somewhat exciting and adventurous. Little did he know how involved he would get in the investigation.

Cannard also shared details of the arrest plan. Marie didn't like the idea of him taking such an active role, while Richard wished he could go along. Cannard assured his wife that there would be adequate police protection, which reminded him of the extra patrols around the house.

"Don't panic" Cannard said, while he explained that over the next few days police officers would be checking the house, all hours of the day, and walking around it with flashlights at night.

Cannard stressed the importance of not mentioning this to anybody. It could jeopardize the investigation and even the family. Everyone understood and went to bed that evening, doing their best to get a good night's rest.

Sunday was anything but relaxing. The stress imposed on the family made them hyper-vigilant. They continuously peered out between the curtains toward the street, were startled each time the phone rang and apprehensive when answering a knock at the door. It was hell and no way to live in the sanctity of your home. Cannard wanted it to end, now!

The first day of the work week was difficult for everyone. Cannard got up and went to the factory like he normally did, but it wasn't easy to act normal, like nothing was bothering him. Marie was left home alone. Cannard constantly worried about her becoming a victim. It never left his mind. There was some comfort in knowing that the police department would be dedicating extra patrols to their house. *Maybe I should have let a police officer stay at the house,* he thought to himself several times during the day.

It was no different for Richard and Anice. Their two-block walk to school was nerve-wracking. Every snow-crunching step seemed to be in slow motion. They continuously looked in all directions, forward, side-to-side and behind to make sure they weren't being followed.

It was somewhat of an adrenaline rush for Richard. How awesome, he thought, it would be if he saw, chased down, and apprehended those responsible for tormenting his family. On the outside, Anice shared her brother's feelings, but inside she couldn't wait for this to end. In their classrooms they constantly thought about it and often "zoned out," not paying attention to the lectures.

Inside the Green Bay Police Department, Lt. Burke and Det. Delloye shared the case with the well known and experienced police chief, Thomas Hawley. Hawley, like he normally did, sat back and listened, taking it all in. The chief agreed, considering the lack of legitimate leads to follow up on, that the best possible chance of apprehending the extortionists would be to go through with the "drop".

Information sharing at the police department between patrol and detectives was on a need-to-know basis. To protect the integrity of the investigation, Chief Hawley agreed that the planned take-down would be kept a secret. They would

The former home of the Cannard family at 136 S. Roosevelt Road. Both letters from the Triangle Club were sent here. (Photo by Mike R. Knetzger.)

tell the patrol division the reason for the extra patrols, but the other plans wouldn't be mentioned. Unknown to them, some patrol officers had already caught wind of the scheduled drop and were planning on taking part in the apprehension. The notoriety alone, of participating in such an arrest, was worth the risk.

Marie spent a long Monday alone at home. Cannard called frequently to make sure she was okay. Seeing a squad car slowly drive by and even stop in front of the house temporarily calmed her nerves. But the anxiety returned as soon as they left.

Richard and Anice arrived home from school and hurried inside to make sure their mom was okay. Her presence comforted them a bit and they patiently waited for their father.

Cannard arrived home from work in the early evening and took a deep breath while grabbing the mail. No other Triangle Club letters were received and the Cannards were together again. Just when they thought it was time to relax and, for now, believed everything was going to be okay…the phone rang, startling them. They sensed something wasn't right.

"Hello, Cannards" answered Cannard. A chill crawled up his neck.

"Is this Mr. Cannard?" the unidentified caller asked.

"Yes, this is him," replied Cannard.

"Tap. Tap. Tap. Click." The phone went dead.

"Hello? Hello?" said Cannard, but there was no response.

Cannard didn't know what to make of this and he would be sure to mention it to Detective Delloye a few hours from now. He told Marie what had just happened. It reminded her of a similar call she had received earlier in the afternoon and forgot to mention. She didn't know what to make of it at the time, but they now became suspicious of both calls. Cannard thought to himself: *Was it the blackmailers ensuring that I was home?*

About an hour later, Cannard was preparing to sit down with his family for dinner. He inquired with Marie, Richard and Anice to make sure nothing suspicious was seen by any of them throughout the day. Nobody had anything else to report and they began to eat. A bit nervous, Cannard didn't eat much and their meal was interrupted by another phone call. Initially, Cannard didn't move and refused to answer it. They stared, silently at each other and the tension could be felt in the air. Overriding the inner voice that told him not to answer it, Cannard thought it might be the police calling to confirm their arrival for the drop later on.

Cannard slowly rose to his feet and walked toward the phone. He exhaled nervously and raised the receiver to his right ear.

"Hello?" said Cannard, this time not offering his last name.

"Mr. Cannard?" the male caller asked; a different voice than the previous one.

Cannard swallowed hard and replied, "Yes."

"Tap. Tap. Tap." Before the caller hung up, Cannard pleaded and asked, "Why? Why are you doing this to us?"

"Click," the phone disconnected.

Cannard immediately phoned the police department and spoke with Det. Delloye. He told him about the phone calls. Delloye assured him that he and Burke would respond right away.

Cannard looked out the front window and didn't see anyone or anything suspicious. He rejoined his family at the dinner table and waited for the detectives to arrive. They all hoped it would be the last call.

Within 30 minutes, Delloye and Burke arrived, bringing a uniformed officer with them. The officer would remain at the residence until the Triangle Club was arrested.

Cannard told Delloye and Burke about all three suspicious phone calls. They agreed that the calls were strange and deduced that the three taps could signify the three points of a triangle. Hence, members of the Triangle Club probably placed the calls.

Delloye had also brought the bait money with him. The lunch-sized paper bag was stuffed with crumpled up newspaper made to look like it was filled with the money. The police officers reviewed and rehearsed the plan with Cannard. Feeling comfortable with it, Delloye and Burke stepped outside and allowed him some privacy with his family.

"I love you," said Cannard while embracing his wife. Richard and Anice looked on, praying that their dad would return soon.

"I love you, Dad," said Richard and Anice while hugging him.

"Be strong. I'll be home real soon," Cannard said, doing his best to reassure and comfort them.

"We will finally know who this Triangle Club is…" he said, going out the front door. The door closed slowly behind him and he walked into the dark of night.

Cannard climbed behind the wheel of his Hudson and started it. The bait "money" sat beside him on the front passenger seat. Delloye and Burke laid low in the back. Underneath his black overcoat, Delloye concealed a sawed-off shotgun and a holstered .32 caliber Luger pistol. Hopefully all would go smooth and he wouldn't have to use these tools of the trade. Just in case, Burke also was armed with a .32 caliber pistol of his own.

Cannard drove north to E. Walnut Street and turned right, driving two blocks to N. Baird Street. He turned left and glanced to his right, looking at East High School and City Stadium as he passed by. A few blocks north he arrived at Willow Street and turned right, heading towards Hwy. 78. He started watching for the lighted box. Not finding it at the city limits, he continued into the Town of Preble. A mile or so from the city Willow Street met up with Hwy. 78 and he veered left.

"I'm on 78," said Cannard.

"Let us know when you see the lighted box." replied Delloye.

"Pay attention to the rear," Burke said. "Let us know if you think anybody is following us."

Cannard constantly looked from side-to-side, while also checking behind him in his rear view mirror. He saw headlights some distance behind him but assumed it was just another ordinary motorist. He turned his attention back toward the road and now, about five miles from the city, Cannard saw some strange lights to his left. Getting closer, he realized that it was what he was looking for.

"I see the box" said Cannard, "Right across the street from Shorty Van Pee's Soda Parlor".

"Okay, let's do it," said Delloye. "Be careful, William."

Meanwhile, the headlights behind them went dark. Lieutenant William Walters and Officer Oran Wall occupied this vehicle. Word of the drop had gotten back to them, probably from the front desk officer who may have overheard the conversation Saturday evening. Armed with their pistols and a shotgun, they wanted to take part in the arrest, or at the very least, witness it. Their failure to notify Burke and Delloye would be a fatal error. They, too, saw the lighted box ahead and stopped alongside the road. They exited and approached the area, walking west.

"Wasn't Delaney supposed to join us?" asked Wall, realizing that the two of them might not be enough if things went wrong.

"Yeah, but there was a change of plans. He's back on his beat," responded Walters.

"I thought he got a replacement, some new officer?" said Wall, dumbfounded.

"Who knows? If so, then I guess they're both walking the beat tonight," replied Walters, while the two officers approached the box.

A Dark Main Street Alley

Relegated to his Main Street beat, Officer Simon Delaney's emergency replacement officer didn't show. At least that's what he thought was the case. Pulling doors was the beat officer's lot — a necessary function that helped prevent burglaries and, on occasion, discover or interrupt one in progress. Patrol officers accepted the rather mundane task and business owners appreciated it.

With flashlight in hand, Delaney sloshed through the puddles of melting snow wondering how the Triangle Club apprehension would go down. His thoughts were interrupted when he came across some excitement of his own.

"Who the heck is that?" Delaney thought to himself seeing a figure walking in the dark alley toward him holding a bright flashlight. The blinding light prohibited Delaney from seeing the person.

"Go ahead, break in," Delaney silently encouraged the prowler to enter and burglarize the first open door he found. He yanked door after door and upon getting closer to Delaney, found one open.

Delaney moved ahead and concealed himself along the door frame, waiting for his foe to exit.

"Halt! Hands up! Hands up!" Delaney ordered, pointing his revolver at the figure.

Startled, the prowler jumped back and threw his hands in the air and yelled, "I'm a police officer! A police officer!"

Taken back by this comment, Delaney paused for a moment and asked, "Where is your uniform? What is your name?"

A quivering, nervous voice replied, "Geyer, James Geyer… My uniform…I haven't got it yet…I just started…"

"Yeah, right. Don't move!" ordered Delaney as he circled behind the suspect and patted him down. Feeling a holstered weapon, Delaney removed and secured the revolver in his waistline.

"Put your hands behind your back!" commanded Delaney and the suspect complied. The handcuffs ratcheted around each wrist and the man was in custody.

"Walk with me to the jail," said Delaney and the man did, explaining that he had bought the gun for police work. The man insisted that he was a police officer and even cited Chief Hawley as his boss. Everybody knew Chief Hawley and his pleas fell on deaf ears.

His head hung low in disbelief, the suspect willingly walked into the jail cell and the iron bars slammed shut behind him. He sat on the planks, the bed hung from the wall by chains, praying that the desk captain would soon recognize him.

Delaney walked upstairs into the police department and began his report.

The Drop

Cannard grabbed the paper bag and slowly brought the Hudson to a stop alongside the marked fence post, which was part of a farm field. Cannard exited, dropped the bag in the box, hurried back inside his car and drove on.

Shorty Van Pee's sold more than just soda. Chicken was their specialty along with the prohibited brew on the side. It was a perfect location for the Triangle Club to watch their goods arrive.

Cannard drove ahead a few hundred feet, turned around, and Delloye stepped out. The headlamps silhouetted Delloye while he walked along the shoulder in the snow-covered field. The moderate temperature and clear skies allowed the ambient moonlight to reflect off the snow and help him see. Delloye gripped his sawed-off shotgun. He was within 150 feet of the fence post and concealed himself as best he could in the dormant brush. He focused on the lighted box and watched for any movement near it. The lights from the box diminished his night vision and he had trouble focusing beyond it. It was 9:00 p.m., right on time.

Wall and Walters had already hidden themselves in the brush and crept forward to get a closer look.

"Hey!" whispered Walters, trying to get Wall's attention. "Look, just past the post, to your left. There he is."

Wall also saw the figure, lowered in the brush. They slowly moved towards it, readying themselves to take down the Triangle Club.

Delloye saw them approaching and prepared himself for the arrest. He stood up and took aim. Peering down the front sight, he had his bead on the leader, whose figure was somewhat obscured by the light illuminating from the box. He waited for the right moment to announce himself. He wanted them to reach the box, grab the bait and complete the crime before making the arrest. That would make it a solid case.

Wall and Walters glanced at the lighted box while they walked past it, closing in on Delloye. Burke and Cannard were too far away to see what was about to happen next.

"Halt!" shouted Wall, pointing his shotgun at Delloye.

"What the hell?" Delloye thought to himself, believing he had heard, "Hands up!" He opened fire with his shotgun. Pellets streaked toward Walters and Wall, nearly striking them.

Wall returned fire with his shotgun. The fast No, 5 pellets retained their velocity well in the cold air, striking Delloye's left side.

The blasts caught the attention of the patrons inside the soda parlor. Someone immediately placed a call for help to the sheriff's department and deputies were on their way.

Delloye, feeling the pellets embedded in his skin, ran to his right while holding the shotgun across his body. He pumped off his next five rounds over his left shoulder. He didn't aim and hoped to suppress any return fire until he could get to cover. It was ineffective. The blackmailers kept shooting. Delloye winced in pain. More pellets riddled his left side, legs and torso. Delloye dropped the shotgun and drew his pistol.

Wall and Walters gave chase. Running straight at the blackmailer, it was easy for them to hit their moving target. Wall's remaining rounds were devastating. He raised the barrel and planned to finish the Triangle Club off with a head shot. He squeezed the trigger and the blast rocked his shoulder. He racked another round and fired again. The fire breathing from the barrel flashed into the night.

Pellets ripped into the soft tissue of Delloye's face and drove into his head. His skull stopped the penetration into his brain. Delloye slowed and stumbled. He unloaded his Luger in the direction of the shotgun blasts. Blood streaked down his face, pouring into his eyes, over his nose and dripping onto his lips. Tasting blood, he knew he was in trouble. Refusing to quit, he reached the front steps of the farmhouse and forced his way inside. A trail of blood marked his path.

Delloye stumbled into the foyer and into the house. His blood-streaked face frightened the farmer's family sitting in the front room. They screamed and fled, the door slamming behind them. Screaming and running, they startled Walters and Wall. "We're police officers," yelled Wall, telling them to hide inside their vehicle parked on the driveway. The family eagerly complied.

Walters and Wall approached the front door. Breathing heavy, their exhaled breaths could be seen in the cold night air. They stared at each other and nodded. Wall stood to the left of the door and Walters to the right. They avoided the center of the door, the "fatal funnel," that anybody could shoot through. They raised their guns, prepared to destroy the blackmailer hidden inside. Walters reached for the door and suddenly it flew open.

"Look out!" shouted Wall. Startled, Walters leaped back and raised his gun. The pad of his index finger rested on the trigger. Just a couple of pounds of pressure and it would be all over.

Delloye stumbled out. His arms hung limp along both sides of his body. Blood masked his familiar face. Weak from blood loss he struggled to say his final words.

"I guess you've got me, boys," Delloye said and collapsed, face first.

"Holy shit!" said Wall, now realizing they had just likely killed a fellow officer.

"Damn it! Damn it! Damn it!" yelled Walters.

Burke had heard the shotgun blasts and saw the flashes of fire. He sprinted across the field with his gun drawn. He shouted at Walters and Wall. "Police! Police! Hands up!" He slowed to a brisk walk and pointed his weapon at them. "What the hell?" he thought to himself, seeing a policeman's uniform. Recognizing Wall and Walters, he became speechless and stared at Delloye's bloodied and lifeless body.

Life hung in the balance. They didn't waste any time

talking. There would be plenty of time later for that. Wall ran back across the field to his car. Burke and Walters rolled Delloye's limp body onto his back. Delloye's breathing was shallow. At least he was still alive. Burke scooped him by the armpits, while Walters lifted his legs. They carried him to the driveway where Wall had skidded to a stop. The back doors flew open and they carefully laid Delloye on the back seat. Wall sped off, west into the city and not stopping until they had reached St. Mary's Hospital.

Walters could tell that Burke was furious. "What the hell were you thinking?" said Burke, demanding an answer from Walters.

"We just wanted to..." started Walters and Burke interrupted him, "You wanted to take part in the arrest!"

Choked up, Walters replied, "Yes, and we should have told you we were going to be out here...I never thought... thought...that this would happen."

"You're damn right you should have told us! You better pray that Gus doesn't die!"

Burke walked toward the farmhouse to survey the damage. Walters stood, motionless, in disbelief, still having difficulty comprehending what had just happened. He slowly walked towards the frightened family and apologized. He didn't offer many details and assured them somebody would help clean up the bloody mess.

For a few moments, Burke stared at the considerable number of red drops and small puddles of Delloye's blood. The red trail led up the farmhouse steps, inside and back out again where it pooled. Red streaks smeared the white farmhouse door. He knew whose blood it was and there was no evidence to collect at this crime scene.

Walters and Burke walked to Cannard's car. Neither of them said a word. Walters climbed in the back and Burke sat next to Cannard.

"What happened? Did we get them?" asked Cannard

while starting his car.

"No," said Burke. "A terrible mistake has happened. I'll fill you in later."

Cannard could tell that something was wrong. "Where is Det. Delloye?"

"He's shot and on his way to St. Mary's. I don't know if he's going to make it. Stop! Stop at Shorty's!"

Burke and Walters walked inside the soda parlor looking for anybody suspicious. It wasn't very crowded and nobody stood out. If the Triangle Club had been there, they not only watched the shootout, but also had plenty of time to flee.

Burke used their phone and called the police department. All night-shift officers responded to the area to look for any signs of the extortionists. Sheriff's deputies also joined them in the hunt.

Empty handed, they exited and walked across the street to the lighted box. The "bait" money was still there. Upon closer inspection they noticed that the wooden box was from a local company, the Grebel-Jossart Electric Co. Three flashlights were fastened to it, forming the shape of a triangle. A red automobile taillight lens was wired to the center. Burke removed the box and carried it with him into Cannard's car. Walters followed and all three drove into the city.

"We are going to assign an officer to your house," ordered Burke, not giving Cannard a chance to object or even respond. The offer was gladly accepted and the rest of the ride was quiet. Cannard dropped Burke and Walters off at the police department and drove straight home to break the news to family.

Burke stormed into the police department and told Captain Holz what happened. Word had already gotten back to him and he sent Delaney and the rest of the night officers out to look for the blackmailers. Burke prepared to leave for the Delloye residence while Holz, for the first time, walked downstairs to check on Delany's arrest.

"What the hell are you doing in there Geyer?" Holz recognized the newly hired officer, James Geyer and opened the jail cell.

"I tried to tell him — Delaney — that I was an officer and he didn't believe me. I was just checking doors, like I was told to, and he arrested me."

"Unbelievable! How long have you been down here?"

"I don't know. A couple hours."

"Well, ironically, we just had one of our detectives shot up tonight by some patrol officers through yet another case of mistaken identity. Get the hell out of here. Go home and we will talk more about this later. You need to get a uniform, kid."

Geyer agreed and headed for home.

Holz walked upstairs to tell Burke about Delaney's "arrest," but he had already left for the Delloye residence.

Officer James Geyer was one of seven other officers hired in 1928. For some reason, he quit the same year. Whether or not it was because of this incident is unknown.

Surgery #1 — Critical Condition

"Get me a wheelchair! Get me a wheelchair!" yelled Wall while standing at the hospital entrance. "An officer's been shot! He's in that car!" Wall ran back toward the car with the nurse close behind him. He yanked Delloye out of the backseat and plopped him into the wheelchair. The detective was rushed inside, still dripping a trail of blood.

Delloye was taken to room 117. Barely conscious, he wondered to himself if he would live. Thoughts of his wife and seven children filled his mind. He loved his family and profession too much to die. He refused to give up.

"What happened?" asked Dr. DeCock.

"He was shot, several times, with No. 5 buckshot," replied Wall.

"Anybody under arrest?"

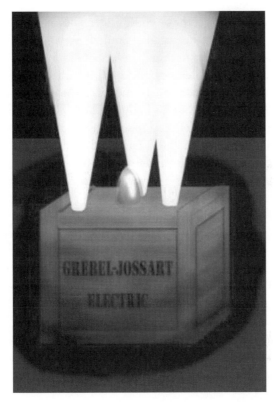

An illustration of the lighted box that Cannard was to place the $1,000 inside or on top of on the evening of Monday, January 9, 1928. The box had been placed on a fence post near Shorty Van Pee's Soda Parlor on Hwy. 78 (present day Hwys. 54-57). (Illustration by Jeremy A. Muraski)

Deliberately withholding the embarrassing truth, Wall replied, "No...no...still looking for them."

"We've got to get the bleeding under control," commented Dr. DeCock while he began his initial assessment. Wall left the room; there was nothing else he could do.

Delloye's unconscious body lay on the bed. He was still breathing and his pulse was good. Each heartbeat pumped more blood throughout his body and out of his wounds. Dr. DeCock and two operating room nurses removed Delloye's clothes. They pulled his arms out of his overcoat and suit and yanked them out from underneath him. The dark clothes had disguised many of the wounds. Taking care not to cut him, his pants' legs were cut from ankle to waist and peeled off. His undershirt was similarly removed. His left leg, waist, and side were so littered with buckshot that it looked like an out-of-control case of bloody, infected measles.

They wiped away the blood to view the hundreds of bloody holes. Delloye's clothing helped slow down the impact of some pellets that were embedded in the surface layers of skin. Other pellets had buried themselves deep in soft, unprotected skin, especially his face and head. Dr. De Cock focused on these more serious wounds. Without anesthesia, Delloye's first surgery began at 10:40 p.m.

A Death Notification?

Burke parked in the driveway of the Delloye residence, 1168 E. Walnut Street. This would be his first potential death notification. He took a deep breath while exiting the driver's seat. Each step up the wooden stairs and onto the porch seemed so loud and slow. He squared off to the front door and knocked.

"Martin?" said Clara Delloye, recognizing him. "What happened? What happened to Gus?" She knew something was wrong.

"I'm so sorry. Gus has been shot. He's at St. Mary's. I will take you there."

Not saying another word, Clara Delloye spun around and headed inside the residence to get her coat and tell the children. She stopped in Lucille's bedroom, the eldest and 19 years old, putting her in charge. Clara Delloye's mind raced. While walking out of the house with Burke, she asked, "Is he going to be okay? How bad is it? Is he going to live?"

To each question Burke answered, "I don't know." A safe, honest and neutral answer. To say that Gus was going to be okay might not have been true. St. Mary's was only a few blocks away and Clara Delloye rushed inside. She would have to wait to see her husband.

"89...90...91...92," Dr. DeCock counted to himself. The metallic sound of each pellet landing in the metal dish could be heard throughout the room. Each one had been dug out of Delloye's skin. Thankfully, none of these wounds were critical. Blood-soaked cloths covered the operating room floor. Delloye's body was covered with bandages. Additional pellets were still buried in his skin and Dr. DeCock was concerned about possible lead poisoning and infection. He administered 3,000 units of tetanus vaccine through a needle in Delloye's left thigh. It was now 11:45 p.m. This hour of pain was enough for any patient to sustain.

Dr. DeCock walked into the waiting area. Seeing his white coat, Clara Delloye rose to her feet.

"Please sit down," said Dr. DeCock, gently.

Clara Delloye hesitated and then placed her hands on the arms of the chair to guide herself down.

"He's stable and going to be okay. He's lucky most of the pellets were shot from a considerable distance. His clothing prevented most of them from deeply penetrating the skin. However, his facial injuries will take a bit longer to heal."

Somewhat relieved, Mrs. Delloye responded, "Okay. Thank God! Thank you, doctor."

"You're welcome. You may go and see him now. He's a bit

drowsy, but awake."

Mrs. Delloye walked the short distance to her husband's room. "What is he going to look like?" she wondered. She walked into the room and gasped, covering her mouth. A bandaged thigh. Bandaged abdomen, left ribs, and arm. Bandaged face and head. He looked like a poorly dressed mummy.

She stood over him, speechless. Tears rolled down her cheeks. He turned and looked at her through tired eyes. His right arm was elevated by a pillow. She squeezed the elevated hand.

"I love you, Gus."

"My love. Everything is going to be okay," Delloye said quietly.

"How did this happen? Who did this to you?"

Not wanting to upset her anymore then she was, Delloye replied, "I will explain more in the morning."

Puzzled by his comment, she stood, waiting to hear more.

"Go home. Be with the kids and tell them that I'll be okay."

She kissed him on the forehead and whispered, "I love you." He watched her walk away and, exhausted, fell asleep.

Tuesday, January 10, 1928

Like the lives of the Delloye and Cannard families, things were hell at the police department the morning following the shooting. Chief Hawley ordered Walters and Wall into his office.

"Sit down!" commanded Hawley.

Without a word, the two officers sat, prepared for the consequences of their actions. Termination was expected. Anything less was a bonus.

In a rare moment, Hawley climbed out of his quiet shell

and yelled. "What the hell were you thinking?" Hawley didn't expect, nor want a response and he continued berating them. "Was this your investigation? Were you asked to participate? Were you told to help?"

Walters and Wall continued to listen and just waited to here the words: "You're fired!" Their eyes followed Hawley from side to side while he paced in front of them.

"No! No! No! It wasn't your investigation! You weren't asked to help! You weren't told to help!"

Hawley slammed a copy of the municipal code on his desk. "This book gives me the authority to terminate you for this." Hawley paused and stared at them. "But, I'm not going to do that. Nothing can change what happened to Gus and thankfully he's going to live. Mark my words, if either of you do anything remotely close to this again or as stupid, I will have your badge! Get the hell out of my office!" Hawley sat back down behind his desk.

It was obvious that Hawley was done. Walters and Wall couldn't believe that they were going to keep their jobs. They apologized and asked if there was anything they could do. Hawley replied, "Go find that Triangle Club." The two officers walked out.

Amazing. Unbelievable. Incompetent. Depending on one's perspective, these words accurately described the shoot-out between officers. Hawley spent the rest of his morning on damage control, doing the best he could to explain why this happened, while at the same time trying to minimize the embarrassment. The mayor's office, lawyers and reporters all wanted a story.

Hawley had a lengthy discussion with Mayor McGillion. They both recognized that mistakes were made and an examination of the current communications and information sharing between detectives and patrol officers needed to be done. McGillion had also supported keeping Walters and Wall on the job. Firing them would only exasperate things.

Dealing with the mayor was the easier part of Hawley's day. Several curbstone lawyers were upset that the Green Bay police officers had gone outside their jurisdiction to make an arrest. Many believed that the Green Bay police didn't have authority to make an arrest in the Town of Preble, which was patrolled by the sheriff's department. The chief disagreed, citing that the original crime had occurred in the city. Unsatisfied with Hawley's position, the lawyers took their complaints to the mayor's office.

The mayor was miffed that lawyers would bring up such a petty issue. He had a seriously wounded police officer in the hospital and some of the "finest" legal minds wanted to argue jurisdiction. He took them to task and made it very clear that he was behind his officers 100 percent. He used the newspapers to his advantage, explaining that "police officers have the power of constable. No one has the right to complain except the blackmailer." He also made appeals to logic and proposed the following scenario:

"Supposing the criminal had actually been arrested by the police. No doubt his lawyers would raise the question to the legality of the arrest. Even though the court might have held the arrest was illegal, the sheriff could be standing by and immediately re-arrest him upon his release. Furthermore, no one thinks for a minute if a man was being murdered just outside the city that the police would refuse to do anything about it because it was outside of their jurisdiction. No one in this matter has the right to complain excepting the criminal and his complaint would be like that of one robber complaining against another who shot him as they both tried to rob the same house."

Rebuffed, the lawyers went away and no further legal issues arose.

The followup investigation was in full swing. Resident fingerprints expert, Detective Otto Cronce, examined the wooden box for evidence. He dusted it for latent prints and didn't find any. The only lead the box provided was the name written on it, the Grebel-Jossart Electric Co.

Detective Burke interviewed V.E. Grebel, one owner of the electric company, about the origin of the box. Grebel explained that it had belonged to them at one time and was probably used for re-delivering goods over the holidays. Anybody could have used it. It was probably someone from the area or who had local connections. Burke got the names of all employees of the company and checked their backgrounds. No additional leads were generated.

Burke also visited the Cannards, who now were getting used to having a police officer live with them. They were still shaken up by this and it would take several months for things to return to normal. The focus now was to make sure that the Cannards were safe and, of course, to arrest the blackmailers, whoever they were. The family didn't have an extra bed and the officer was relegated to the couch, a location he would become accustomed to over the next couple of weeks.

Cannard apologized to Burke for what had happened and at times blamed himself for Delloye's pain. It didn't help him deal with some of his guilt when he then found out what really happened to Delloye.

"This wouldn't have happened if I hadn't gone to the police department," he said.

"Mr. Cannard, don't blame yourself," replied Burke. "Had you not brought this to our attention the end result could have been even worse. You, your wife, even your children could've have wound up dead. For all we know, our mistake saved your lives. You did the right thing…"

More Shotgun Pellets…

"How are you this morning Mr. Delloye?" asked the nurse.

"I feel fairly well," replied Delloye. "But it feels real tight behind my left ear."

The nurse examined the area and noticed it was swollen and discolored. Figuring a pellet was lodged there, she left the room to get Dr. DeCock.

DeCock and a colleague, Dr. Kelly, walked in a few minutes later. They examined Delloye behind his left ear and agreed with the nurse's assessment.

"Mr. Delloye, there is probably a pellet lodged behind your left ear. It's hard to tell for sure because of the swelling. When that subsides in the next day or two, we will take a closer look."

The doctors looked at the healing wounds along the left side of Delloye's body. He winced and moaned in pain when the bandages were pulled away. The wounds were cleaned and dressed again. Everything appeared to be healing well. The doctors walked out, passing by Mrs. Delloye and Burke who arrived to visit.

Clara Delloye stood alongside her husband and prayed that he would come home soon. The kids were worried. She was worried. They needed him. She again asked what had happened. Burke and Delloye glanced at each other and began to tell the story.

Burke began, "We were right on time and the drop went as planned. But we didn't know that two other officers were following us. They wanted to take part in the arrest. Gus waited in the field for the Triangle Club to arrive. He saw two people walking towards him in the dark…"

Delloye interjected, "And I thought it was them, the guys we were looking for. As they got closer to me, they yelled something, which may have been, 'Halt!' But I took it for, 'Hands up!' I just started shooting…"

"The officers shot back at Gus and the rest is history," concluded Burke.

"You've got to be kidding me!" demanded Mrs. Delloye. "Who were these officers?"

"Walters and Wall," replied Burke, "and they feel terrible

about it."

Frustrated she said, "So, this was completely avoidable, wasn't it? Where are the…the thugs, the ones who wrote the letter?"

"We are still working on that." Burke couldn't bear to tell her that there weren't any leads.

"It's okay, dear. I will be okay. It was a terrible accident," said Delloye, trying to comfort her.

Not only was she angry that her husband had been shot, but more frustrated to know how it happened. Her tearful eyes spoke for themselves.

Mrs. Delloye visited again later and brought the children with her. All of them were saddened and shocked by what had happened to their father. It was a moment frozen in time that they would never forget. It was stressful enough knowing that he could get shot in the line of duty and now it was reality. They prayed it would never happen again and longed for their father, affectionately called "Papa," to come home. The house wasn't the same without him. Each passing day seemed to last forever and it would be weeks before their wishes would come true.

Burke returned to the police department and sat at his desk. He completed his reports and struggled with what to do next, especially without any legitimate or promising leads. He needed any help he could get. Then the obvious jumped out at him. The letters had been sent through the mail and nobody had yet tried to trace them.

Burke phoned the postal inspector's office and they sent an investigator who arrived later in the afternoon. The letters and envelopes were examined and compared to other known cases. The handwritten address, typewritten font and style and letter and word spacing were all studied. The return address, had it existed, would have provided the ultimate lead. Their assistance was appreciated, but they failed to generate any significant information.

Burke again found himself at his desk. Exhausted, he sat back, slouched in his chair and stared at the ceiling. The desk officer's voice snapped him out of it.

"Burke. Phone call for you. Somebody who said they saw the box before you guys arrived."

"Detective Burke," he answered, hoping this one call would break the case.

"Hello, detective. I read what happened and just wanted to let you know that my wife and I saw the box, the lighted box, on the fence post while we were on our way home from Bay Settlement Monday night. It had three white lights with a red light in the center."

Burke listened intently and took notes.

The caller continued, "I was going to stop and take a look at it, but for whatever reason I decided not to and drove on."

"What time did you see it?"

"I don't recall exactly. It was dark, sometime before 9 p.m."

"Did you see anybody else by the box?"

"No, nobody. It had already been placed there."

"Have you heard of the Triangle Club or anybody talking about them?"

"Nope, never heard of them. I really didn't make anything of it until I heard what happened to Detective Delloye. I'm very sorry that I can't be of anymore help."

Burke noted the man's name and thanked him for calling.

Ironically, a second call was received a few moments later. Burke listened to another male caller who had seen the lighted box.

"Myself and my girlfriend were driving east and right by Shorty's, across the street, we saw the lighted box. My girlfriend suggested we stop and look, but we were in a hurry and drove on. Maybe I should have listened to her?"

Burke asked the same followup questions, trying to establish a timeframe or learning anything else about the Triangle Club. He didn't get any new information and neither of these calls generated significant leads.

That evening at the Cannard residence was interesting, to say the least. To William and Marie Cannard, their uniformed houseguest was a necessity. To Anice, it was a bit odd having a police officer live with them. But to Richard it was exciting. What could have been heard on a thrilling radio show was happening in his house. He was living it. The ending would be a mystery and leave the listener sitting on the edge of their seat. Whatever the conclusion, Richard wanted to be a part of it.

Wednesday, January 11, 1928 — Surgery No. 2

Just as fast as the bullets flew and ripped into Delloye's skin, the leads in the case vanished. There simply wasn't much to go on. They had one opportunity to apprehend the Triangle Club and that had been lost in the dark on Hwy. 78. All members of the police and sheriff's departments made it their goal to apprehend the extortionists. A lofty goal, especially when you don't know who you're looking for. Many inquiries were made with known criminals and vagrants to no avail. Agencies throughout the state were also notified. All that could be done now was to sit back and wait.

Delloye watched the gas mask cover his nose and mouth. He peacefully went to sleep and endured his second surgery. It was now 8:45 a.m and for the next hour Dr. DeCock removed all the bandages to examine the healing wounds and dig out any additional pellets buried in Delloye's skin.

The doctor worked from the head down. Each apparent wound was probed for a pellet. Partially healed skin was separated with a sterile tweezers. Blood and pus oozed out. Each dark colored pellet was dug out. The sharp tips of the tweezers were pushed into the wound along each side of the pellet. With a firm grip, it was pulled out and the skin closed, partially sealing the hole. This tedious process happened at least sixty-five more times along Delloye's head, face, arm, abdomen, hip and leg. A cold and soothing feeling came upon the wounds when Mercuro Chrome, an antiseptic, was dabbed on each one to prevent infection. Just to make sure, another three thousand units of tetanus were injected into his left thigh. The end of this procedure brought the total pellet count to 157.

I don't know anything about it... — Det. Martin Burke

The forty-eight hours of media attention to this case gave the Cannards a sort of celebrity status. All of their relatives, especially Arthur Cannard, wanted to know more. Arthur, knowing that he was probably the intended target, became wary of all unfamiliar people who walked into his bank. Looking over his shoulder became a temporary way of life.

At work, William Cannard was bombarded with questions and he re-told the story many times. He became so tired of repeating himself that each time he told a shortened version. Richard and Anice were given similar attention at school. It was neat at first, but the constant inquiries became overwhelming. When asked by reporters for additional comment on the case, Cannard responded, "There has been too much publicity already." Revisiting the details over and over again made recovery that much more difficult.

The Cannards visited Delloye in the hospital and thanked him for his efforts. They shared their sympathies for his plight. True to form, Delloye didn't expect any of this, citing that he was only doing his job.

Over the next seventy-two hours, no new leads developed in the case. The story about Delaney arresting Geyer had made the papers and Hawley wasn't happy about it. A newspaper reporter, standing in Hawley's office asked about the Delaney and Geyer story. Burke was also present and listened intently. In response, Chief Hawley sat silently, refusing to answer, while taking a critical look at his cigar and slowly bringing it to his lips. The reporter turned toward Burke, who replied, "I don't know a thing about it."

Unable to keep this story under the table, the police and fire commission caught wind of it and demanded an explanation from Hawley. On the evening of the 13th, the commission met with Hawley in the mayor's office. In public, they may have appeared outraged, embarrassed, or even disgusted over these new developments, but behind closed doors it was probably a different story. Rumors had spread throughout the community and some even believed that Delaney had actually arrested one of now infamous Triangle Club members. Amidst occasional laughter and sarcasm, the chief did his best to set the record straight. He insisted that most of the story was correct except that nobody was sent to relieve Delaney and nobody was arrested. Had somebody been arrested, Hawley surmised, the desk officer at the station would have been aware of it. With that off the table, Hawley then explained to the commission, without making his department look incompetent, what exactly went wrong during the attempted apprehension of the blackmailers. All agreed it was tragic and certain measures yet to be determined needed to be put into place to prevent this from ever happening again.

Saturday, January 14, 1928 — Surgery No. 3

In the interim, Delloye's hospital life, unlike the shooting that put him there, became somewhat predictable. Nurses monitored him throughout the day and night. They regularly checked vital signs and paid attention to any signs of infection. Delloye arose earlier each morning to stiffness in various areas along the left side of his body. The slightest move caused discomfort and lying still, although uncomfortable at times, was preferred. Each day seemed to bring on different aches and pains. While some wounds began to heal, others yet to be noticed bothered him. The morning sponge bath helped sooth some of the burning and also gave nurses the chance to notice pellets still lodged in his body. Delloye would endure the pain, absent anesthesia, of the occasional pellet being dug out. However, each passing day revealed more and more pellets that had been missed during the first two surgeries. A third and final surgery was deemed necessary.

Delloye's third procedure of the week wasn't much unlike his first two. The same gas mask put him to sleep. The same sterilized tweezers were used to separate skin, dig into it and remove more pellets. Near the end of this twenty-five minute procedure, Dr. DeCock took a final look and believed he had finally removed all of them. More mercurochrome was dabbed on each wound to prevent infection at the site. A count of the pellets in the dish along Delloye's bedside revealed to the doctor that he had removed twenty more, about one per minute. This brought the total count to at least 177. The final tally didn't include the occasional one that was plucked out of Delloye in the days preceding this surgery. The only other thing that this procedure changed was the placement of bandages on his body. Another 1,500 units of tetanus vaccine were injected to help ensure the doctor that Delloye would make a full and uneventful recovery. The hospital remained his home.

The end of this week couldn't come fast enough for everybody involved. Hawley needed to get away from the constant inquiries. Burke needed time to sit back and make a complete analysis of the case. Their current strategy of the occasional inquiry wasn't working and he needed to come up with a different course of action. Hopefully the weekend alone would develop some leads. The Cannards were becoming accustomed to their houseguest who spent much of his time on the sofa. The officer occasionally made his rounds around the house, both inside and out. Any initial fascination with the case was changed by the constant, uneventful monotony and boredom. They became numb to the occasional phone call and no other Triangle Club letters were received.

Monday, January 16, 1928

First thing in the morning, Hawley and Burke sat down to discuss the case. Burke laid out the dirty extortion letters on the chief's desk. They were permanently stained with black fingerprint dust.

Burke began, "Two envelopes and two letters, both typed with the same machine; neither had a return address. The postal inspectors haven't had any similar cases." Burke paused and glanced at Hawley, who, with a cigar clinched in between his teeth, nodded, encouraging him to continue.

"The Cannards don't have any suspects in mind and have never heard of the Triangle Club and, frankly, neither have we. Outside of the obvious motive being money, no other motives are apparent. The letter was probably intended for Cannard's brother, the banker. Cronce dusted the box for prints and found none... Damn it! Chief, we don't have a damn thing to go on!"

Hawley broke his silence and asked, "What about the witnesses, anymore from them?"

"Nothing new. No other witnesses have come forward. The two that did, they saw the lighted box, but didn't see who put it there."

"Did the Cannards see anything suspicious around the house lately?"

Burke replied, "Nothing, nothing at all. Everything seems normal at their place. If they are being watched, we don't know it."

"Well then," said Hawley, "sounds like it's time to be creative."

They tossed around some ideas and came up with a plan

that some would consider radical, others dangerous and a few would call ingenious.

"Do you think the Cannards will agree to us using their children as decoys?" asked Burke, doubting they would.

"We won't know till we ask them," replied Hawley.

"I'll meet with them right away and let you know." Burke stood up to leave and began walking out of Hawley's office when the chief interrupted his departure.

"Hey, Burke, one more thing, the mayor approved a $100 reward for information leading to the arrest of these black-mailers. It will hit the papers tomorrow and maybe that will generate some tips."

"It can't hurt," commented Burke, leaving the office and heading for the Cannard home.

Burke rolled into the driveway not expecting the family to agree to their crazy plan. The uniformed officer let him inside. Burke asked him for an update and there was nothing new to report. All was normal and he met with the family in the front room.

Burke began, "Unless you have something new, we haven't got any more leads."

"No nothing," replied Cannard. "Everything has been normal around here. No phone calls, no letters and no suspicious people. What do you have in mind detective?"

"We've come up with an idea that might work…it's a long shot, but it could give us a break in the case." They all sat silently and waited for Burke to share the elaborate plan. "We would like to try using Richard and Anice as decoys. The blackmailers already know where you live and for all we know they have been watching the house. Since they never received the money, they might be desperate. We would like to have them…" Burke glanced at Richard and Anice who were staring, waiting for their instructions… "walk the area for a few blocks around the neighborhood. We will have plainclothes officers following. If the blackmailers or any stranger approaches them, the officers will make the arrest." Burke paused and waited for a response.

Marie immediately objected, "Absolutely not! What if they get shot? Are the officers going to prevent that from happening?"

Cannard tried to be rational and although knowing the risks, turned to his kids and asked, "Richard and Anice, what do you think about this?"

"That is the cat's meow! Of course I'll do it!" said Richard. He finally had gotten his wish to be part of that thrilling radio show ending.

Anice, on the other hand, was a bit apprehensive. But she was willing to cooperate and go along with the plan. If it meant the end of this ride, she was willing to take the risk. Marie reluctantly agreed to let her only children participate in this risky plan.

Burke thanked them for their willingness. He would contact them in a day or two and let them know when they wanted to try it. Pleasantly surprised, Burke left the house and drove to the hospital to visit Delloye.

Burke rounded the corner and walked into Room 117. "Holy smokes Gus, you're sitting up!" said Burke, seeing his old friend seated upright for the first time in a week. "That's a good sign. How have you been feeling?"

Delloye replied, "I'm actually feeling a little more comfortable…and I'm ready to get the heck out of here!"

"I hear ya!" replied Burke, "But if you get up and walk away now, with all those bandages on you, they will thinking you're the walking dead."

Delloye laughed and grabbed his left side to minimize the pain caused by his chuckling belly and ribs.

Burke briefed Delloye on the case and shared with him the plan to use the Cannard children as bait. Delloye was also one to be creative and hoped it would work. They talked for awhile and Burke left once the nurses arrived to administer their afternoon care. It was a daunting task for any nurse to monitor and clean the more than 177 wounds scattered throughout his body. It was nothing short of a miracle that the lead pellets and wadding didn't cause infection.

Offer $100 Reward for Clues to Blackmailers — **Green Bay Press-Gazette, July 17, 1928**

Just as Hawley had said, the $100 reward offer was released to reporters. Unfortunately, it was buried on page 19 of the paper, which minimized the number of people that would actually see it. They waited patiently for any new tips.

Burke made arrangements for two officers, wearing plain clothes, to meet him at the Cannard residence at about 6:00 p.m. They wanted to take advantage of the cover of darkness. Burke arrived a few minutes early to make sure the Cannards still wanted to go through with this. They were anxious to get it over with.

Burke explained the simple instructions. "Walk around the neighborhood, a couple blocks in each direction. The uniform officers will be following close behind. If anybody, anybody at all, approaches you, stay calm and wait for the officers to arrive. If they have a weapon, cooperate. If they try to kidnap you, do what it takes to talk your way out of it and buy yourself a couple of seconds. That's all it will take for the officers to get to you. Do either of you have any questions?"

"No!" said Richard, speaking on behalf of both of them while Anice nodded her head in agreement. Richard couldn't wait for them to get started.

With the uniformed officers in tow, Richard and Anice began their trip. They walked north on S. Roosevelt Street to E. Walnut Street and then east toward the high school. They both constantly looked in between passing houses and glanced behind them to make sure the uniformed officers were following. At Baird Street they turned right and headed south toward Doty Street. The large green space in front of the high school would be the perfect location for any blackmailers to conceal themselves. None would make their presence known. They then turned right on Doty and headed west towards S. Roosevelt. The officers kept close enough to watch them, but far enough back and within the shadows of darkness to not give themselves up. Richard and Anice continued scanning from side to side, in front of and behind them. Richard so wished that the blackmailers would approach them! How great it would be to take part in the apprehension. Anice just wanted this over with. Richard's wish would never come true and he would never hear the end of this story. They completed their square and returned to the residence. William Cannard and his wife were cautiously optimistic for any new developments, of which there were none. They were just thankful that their kids walked in the house unharmed.

Disappointed, exhausted and on the verge of giving up, Burke returned to the police department and longed for a break. It was soon becoming a cold case.

Blackmailers Demand $1,000 from Woman — Green Bay Press-Gazette, January 18, 1928

"Holy shit!" Burke exclaimed, seeing the headline on page 1. Could the Triangle Club had struck again in Waupun, 80 miles south of Green Bay? Anything was possible and the demand amount was the same.

Burke read on and the first sentence confirmed that they, at least tried to do the right thing, deliver a bogus bundle of money, wait for the blackmailers to arrive and arrest them. Like the Green Bay case, the trap failed. Unlike the Green Bay case, police didn't get into a shootout with each other.

He continued to study the article and noted that the Waupun blackmailers properly selected their target, a wealthy businessman, whom they also threatened to kill if he didn't

Det. Martin Burke, also known as the "walking records department," retired in 1936 after 37 years of service. Det. August "Gus" Delloye reitred in 1956 after a 40-year career. Chief Thomas E. Hawley retired in 1946 after 53 years with the department, 49 of them as chief. (Photos courtesy of the Neville Public Museum of Brown County.)

comply. These ironies were interesting, but if the letter were signed the Triangle Club then a definite link could be established. He anxiously read the text of the printed letter.

"On the 16 or 17 of January you will give us $1,000 or we will take your man for a ride. We will watch you and him and have a way of knowing if you let anyone know; we will blow the big stone in the cemetery into a pile of rock to let you know we are wise and then raise the price to $10,000, which you will be glad to pay. We do not believe in this holding....Think how easy it is to shoot a man in this town after dark and get away."

On the morning of the 19th, Burke brought the article with him and set it on Hawley's desk. Hawley had also read it the night before and it became their first order of business to contact the Waupun Police.

With one simple phone call, Burke's excitement about the letter possibly being sent by the Triangle Club quickly turned to disappointment. The Waupun police informed him that it was a handwritten letter and wasn't signed by the Triangle Club. He also learned that the Waupun letter was crudely written on the back of a handbill and not on a standard 8½ x 11 sheet of paper. If this handwritten letter had been sent by the Triangle Club, they did a clever job of changing their method of operation. No link was established and this potential lead, like the others, fizzled.

Over the next four days, Delloye's condition continued to improve. He stood for the first time in ten days and, understandably, walked with a limp. He began to walk a little bit each day and every step was one step closer to going home. Instead of standing by his bed during her visit, Clara Delloye now walked the halls with her husband. The held hands and talked about the kids or any new developments in the case that she might have heard about.

On the morning of Monday, January 23, 1923, two weeks from the day that Wall shot him, Det. August Delloye got the news he longed for. He was released from the hospital. Many of the wounds were still healing, but the danger of infection was slight.

At 11:25 a.m., Delloye and his wife, hand-in-hand, slowly walked out of St. Mary's Hospital. He still walked with a slight limp. They were picked up at the curb by a squad car and driven home. "Papa" was welcomed with the open arms of his children. He also looked forward to his second favorite thing in life, walking the thin blue line for the Green Bay Police Department.

Delloye returned to work a short time later and continued his streak of never missing a day due to illness. He was greeted with handshakes, pats on the back and words of support from all officers who were happy to have him back. Delloye never held any ill-will towards Walters or Wall, who both continued serving the city of Green Bay. Delloye would never see the Triangle Club brought to justice and the case faded into history.

Conclusion

Life at the Cannard residence didn't return to normal until April. The family always believed, and still do today, that the blackmailers, like the police, had the wrong man. The letters were probably intended for Arthur Cannard, the banker. Seven years later, after both Richard and Anice were married and out of the house, the Cannards sold it and moved out of the area.

We will probably never know the true identity of the Triangle Club. The physical evidence and police records are destroyed and all the witnesses, except for one, are deceased. However, research has revealed a theory that supports a "person of interest" who might have known something about the mysterious Triangle Club letters.

Little did Chief Hawley know at the time of this incident that one of his officers was a "good cop, gone bad." Hired in 1924, Officer Elland "Slim" Delaney may have had the best intentions in mind, serving and protecting the citizens of Green Bay. For some reason, in 1928 his intentions changed and bank robbing became his new trade. In December, Delaney participated in the abduction of Farmer's Exchange Bank cashier Thelis Noel. Three other accomplices from Green Bay and DePere assisted and forced Noel to open the bank vault. Could these people have also been the Triangle Club?

Why the shape of a triangle? Could it have signified the number of people involved in the plot? Slim Delaney had intimate knowledge of the Farmer's Exchange Bank and, at the time of the Triangle Club letters, might he have only known the last name of the intended Cannard bank employee? Delaney was also in the perfect position to make sure the crime was never solved. Indeed, it never was and remains a cold case.

In yet another interesting twist, Officer Oran Wall redeemed himself that very same year when he and another officer discovered nearly $12,000 in stolen currency hidden underneath an automobile seat cushion. This stolen cash had been taken by Slim Delaney and his cohorts during the Farmer's Exchange Bank robbery.

"Couple Slain in Roadhouse" – Green Bay Press-Gazette, May 20, 1930

THE GOLDEN PHEASANT

Slash! Both arms swung in the air again to the right, hands gripped angrily on the hatchet handle.

And again. Slash!

The full force of the blade struck between John Van Veghel's eyes, blood splattering behind the bed. The killer drove the corn sickle deep into Van Vegal's skull.

His brown eyes weren't even open yet. Never had a chance.

But it didn't stop.

Plain white walls took on more and more of a horrific red tinge with every slam, rip and tear into Van Veghel's face and head. Eventually his legs slid limply out from under the covers, his feet thumping to the floor in an oddly grotesque position.

The position of death at age 36.

Lucille Birdsall's eyes met her killer from the beginning and until the end. She was awakened by the ripping into John, known to her and friends as Jack. Lucille was Jack's new love, along with her 5-yr-old daughter, Betty Jane. As a pretty 24-year-old, wanted by many, her life was stolen presumably on Monday, May 19, 1930.

The hatchet murder of Van Veghel and Birdsall remains one of the most gruesome crimes in the history of Titletown. The killer was never captured or if he was, never retained for any length of time and charged.

A crime of passion to some, a burglary gone bad to others. Regardless, it was ugly and someone got away with making

2015 Willow St. the tomb of John and Lucille. This was the Golden Pheasant Inn, a roadhouse where John was the proprietor and Lucille was a cook and waitress.

Norb Van Beckum was 13 years old at the time, an 8th grader at St. Willebrord's. Uncle Jack (John) was his mom's brother. It was barely 8 a.m. Tuesday morning, May 20. Norb was sitting at his desk with an English book open, thinking about the upcoming summer break.

Big chicken dinners on Saturdays at Uncle Jack's Golden Pheasant. Norb loved that. It was the Depression and money was hard to come by. But 75 cents brought a chicken dinner made by Lucille with all the fixin's.

It was not to be, not that summer. No more chicken dinners with Uncle Jack.

Norb looked up to find the principal nun standing in front of him. "Norb, I need you and your brother to go home right away. Your mother needs you," said the nun, no expression.

Gulp. Norb swallowed the little bit of spit in his mouth and took in air at the same time. Something felt wrong, very wrong. Mom had never sent for them before. A chill crawled slowly through his shoulders and then down his spine. "Yes ma'am." He shivered.

They began the walk home. His brother was in seventh grade, just a year younger. Unlikely at that age, but Norb put a hand on his brother's shoulder as they made their way through the front door.

"Uncle Jack was killed, most likely Sunday night but they just found him today," said Mrs. Van Beckum, quivering but trying to hold it together for her boys. She sat on one end of their tan family sofa, wearing a light blue dress, trying to answer the questions of her children, lined up on the end.

The Golden Pheasant

Norb's grandparents had taken a drive by the Golden Pheasant on Monday. "Uncle Jack's car was there but the place was closed. They thought maybe Uncle Jack had gotten word that the Feds were in town and closed up," said Norb.

These were the days of Prohibition. The Golden Pheasant was just north of the red light district. Brothels abounded, the two most well known were Happy Hanson's and Ma Peers, both near the Pheasant. Ten dollars bought much in those days and it was everywhere.

The Golden Pheasant was a roadhouse where locals and visitors could get a bootleg ale and try their luck at slot machines, both quarter and dime slots. The struggles of day-to-day life in 1930 were lost behind the doors of the Pheasant.

Uncle Jack had suffered some losses with a couple of recent slot machine burglaries but he would rather turn his head than face the danger of intruders. Not worth it. He was a businessman who understood loss and gain. Life meant everything to John Van Veghel.

He had encountered death early in life. Too early.

The great flu epidemic hit Titletown in 1916 and Van Veghel lost his wife. She was the first victim of the epidemic in this area. Their infant was baptized just in time, only to perish as well.

John Van Veghel found himself a widower at age twenty-two. Family say that is what made him the serious business-man that he became. Facing death at such an early age brought out focus in another area, that of business.

He had just helped his brother, Walter, establish a "soft drink" saloon at 1215 Main St. Jack was a respected business-man and was not known to attract enemies.

At 5'11, brown hair and brown eyes, he walked with confidence not only at Golden Pheasant but through town.

His gray 1929 Chevrolet was parked in front of the Golden Pheasant on Monday but there was no movement inside.

First the ice man called, but got no answer.

Then the baker. No answer. Golden Pheasant was known

for its hamburgers, of which Lucille was a cook. They went through dozens of buns each week and the baker brought them fresh. Odd not to get an answer with Jack's vehicle parked outside.

"My dad, Fred, he threw pebbles at the window. He was a meter reader for Wisconsin Public Service and couldn't get his attention," said Van Beckum.

One pebble. Two. Then a handful.

Still no answer.

Concern grew through the day. Van Veghel was a worker. He liked to be open. He had the slots, not for his own enjoyment, but to make money. Before operating the Golden Pheasant, John had started Van's Saloon at the northeast corner of George and Main streets.

"He was all business. In those days people were," said Norb. "There was a dance hall next to the bar and he had the best chicken."

Norb remembered spending many weekend nights enjoying chicken with Uncle Jack, while Lucille cooked in the kitchen. She had been married eight years before at the age of sixteen to Frank Kupsack. They had a daughter together but it didn't work out.

Kupsack was a latherer by trade and wanted to move Lucille and the baby from Illinois to Milwaukee where he could increase his pay from 35 cents an hour to $1.10 but she fought the idea.

"I kept telling her, Lucille, we will never get anywhere this way, but she wouldn't have it," Kupsack was heard to say. He said they were not very good friends after the divorce.

After the separation, Birdsall moved to Sturgeon Bay near her parents and eventually came to Green Bay. She then went to work for Van Veghel, leaving her daughter, Betty Jane, with her parents for proper care.

She had a way of talking to people that brought life to the room, wherever she was. However, sometime between 4 and 6 a.m. on Monday, May 19th, she stared into the eyes of death and lost. The color of those eyes was never to be known…

Victims Found in Bed, Heads Mashed — Green Bay Press-Gazette, May 20, 1930

Slash! And again the hatchet sliced into the bone of Van Veghel's skull.

It was 1:30 a.m. and Irene Clowry was the other waitress working with Lucille. "Can I help you with anything else?" asked Irene as she watched Birdsall wipe the back grill.

"No, I'll be retiring soon, but thanks, hon," said Lucille, always with a smile and soft tone.

That smile and the soft tones would turn to anguish and shrieks in the hours that followed.

Birdsall was in bed with Van Veghel in his room, which was right off the bar on the first level of the Golden Pheasant. She stayed in the upstairs loft. White sheets held them both in a double bed.

The scene at the Golden Pheasant Restaurant, where the murders took place. (Photo courtesy of the Green Bay Press Gazette.)

It was tucked into the corner beneath the only window, on the south side that faced Willow Street.

Mrs. Cannard Debroux lived next door with her son, Martin Verheygen, nine years old at the time. He would see at that age what no person should ever see in a lifetime.

The bed containing the couple had a metal headboard with bars. Eerie, some would say after the discovery of the couple. The bars should have symbolized the capture of the killer but that would never happen.

A kiss goodnight after Lucille closed up the Pheasant, maybe more, and they were soon sound asleep. John lay on his back. Laying on her right side, Lucille rested her head near his chest with her back along the wall.

Each peaceful breath was one closer to the last. Whatever future they planned together wouldn't be of this world.

Some said that the two had been secretly married because of religious reasons, but there was no confirmation on this. Jack was a good, giving man and the two together were an attractive couple.

She liked his giving side both with others and with her and Betty Jane.

Just before retiring, she had watched as Jack gave a patron and friend a dime to buy cigarettes.

It would be a dime that Eddie Bodart, onetime Green Bay alderman, would owe Jack for eternity. "We were all shocked. Jack never had any enemies," Bodart said of the grisly murders.

It didn't take much to force an entry into the road-house.

A swift kick, a shoulder, a shove is all it took to get in. Suddenly, Van Veghel and Birdsall were fighting for their lives. Van Veghel was hardly awake when he gasped his last breath, his eyes fixated on the ceiling.

With an ax or corn sickle in hand, the killer made his way toward the room. He slowly opened the unlocked door and stared at his prey. His eyes widened and pulse pounded while each step brought him closer.

Deep breath sucked in as he stopped and stood over Van Veghel's head. His left shoulder along the wall, his right arm raised the axe and drove it into Van Veghel's right eye and the bridge of his nose.

Blood splattered and sprayed in all directions, marbling the white walls a gore-filled red discolored the headboard. The pillows and bedding were painted in a way never planned by the couplee.

"It was messy all right. Killing two people like that, there had to be a cause," said Otto Cronce, a Green Bay detective and fingerprint expert who was assigned to the case to assist the Brown County Sheriff's Department. At that time, the Golden Pheasant was part of the town of Preble, which fell under Brown County's jurisdiction. The area later became officially part of Titletown.

In rage, the killer raised the hatchet and drove it in again and again, completely obliterating Van Veghel's face and skull. The victim gasped, raised his hands towards whatever pain registered in his brain and died.

"My grandpa, Peter Van Veghel (twice Brown County Sheriff), said Uncle Jack must have known the killer because he threw his alarm clock at him," said Norb Van Beckum, the victim's nephew.

He never fully awoke and barely moved, according to investigators' notes. The blankets still rested neatly on his chest, like a child who had been tucked in.

Birdsall woke in terror to the sounds of crushing facial bones and skull and the thud of Van Veghel's feet hitting the floor.

"Stop, stop, what are you doing," she screamed with everything in her as she became the next target of the killer's wrath.

"She was meant to be last, to know what was happening. He wanted to get Van Veghel out of the way first," said David Ray, of Neenah. Ray is a well known psychic who conducted a séance at the murder site in 1990. It was one of the last séances he ever conducted. "I never wanted to do it again," said Ray, who is refocused as a psychic entertainer. He uses his gifts to entertain at business parties/conventions and other events.

"No," she shrieked, hyperventilating as the killer swung the hatchet at her head. Her instinct to fight kicked in and she raised her right arm in a feeble attempt to protect herself.

She won. For a moment. He missed and swung through, across his body. He unwound and swung again, slicing her right forearm. Birdsalle grunted with pain, tears and snot matting her cheeks as she tried to escape. But she was trapped between the wall and her killer.

Gritting his teeth with hate, he leaned forward, eyes targeted on Lucille. Practically kneeling on the bed to get in closer, like a hunter sighting his prey, he swung the hatchet again. He struck Lucille underneath her chin and she flailed back.

Wanting an even closer shot, he moved onto the bed, first climbing over John's lifeless legs.

Horror gripped her. Fear froze her but she continued to fight through the pain and through her fear. The killer straddled the victim while her head lay on her pillow, arms extended. She fought to push away the danger that threatened to claim her, staring into the blank eyes of her own would-be killer and that of her love, Jack.

"Why, why," she screamed as her body weakened with each blow. What could she or Jack have done that made them deserving of this?

Unmoved by any pleas of mercy, the killer finished what he came to do.

Focused on her head, he slammed the ax through her eyes, crushing them inward toward her brain.

Inside the Golden Pheasant Restaurant. (Photo courtesy of the Green Bay Press-Gazette.)

Lucille's blood began to mix with John's. Together, but not the way it was supposed to be. Droplets of blood landed on the bedding and on the wall behind and alongside her, spotting the wooden window frame.

Still she fought. Birdsall slid her head off the pillow and along the wall, which may have brought her a few more seconds of life.

He continued plunging the ax like an ice pick and at times swinging it like a corn sickle into her face and head. Her arms went limp and landed on the bed. "So deep were the wounds, they resembled the tearing discharge of a load of buckshot," said Dr. R.C. Buchanan at the time, who was one of two doctors assigned to do the post mortem on both Birdsall and Van Veghel.

"Oh my dear God," he said, visibly shaken at the first sight of the two. The murders were the most brutal he had ever or would ever see in his career.

Life began to leave Birdsall, as her eyes pleaded with her killer. She was no longer able to make any sound.

Out of control, filled with rage, whatever drove this psychopath; it was personal. He would not stop and it didn't take long until death overcame her.

Dead and hardly recognizable, Birdsall now lay partially on her left side, with her right knee slightly bent and arms along side her.

The killer dismounted. He stood at the side of the bed and looked over his kill, which lay in a mass of blood and clots.

Satisfied, he turned away and just as casually as he walked in, walked out.

Police would later find a basement door open and another door on the ground floor closed from the outside with a piece of wood to keep it shut. Likely still dark outside, the killer walked away. The adrenalin of fresh kill, a kill planned, gave him a natural rush. He did not hide behind the building. He did not run. He did not creep along, hoping not to be discovered. This was a killer, unafraid and driven by rage. Taking a deep breath in, he sighed with a glint in eyes that pierced the shadows he was sauntering through.

"Easy," he chuckled, still breathing rapidly. His mood turned from celebratory back to angry. "Bastard," he grunted out, his teeth still clenched and his nostrils flared. "Not gonna take my girl. Not ever again."

He continued to make his way, passing a gray house to the north. He stopped. There was movement in the house. He stood silently, like a hunter waiting for the noise of prey. Rolling back on his heels, he took three steps backward. Eyes focused, he looked at the living room window of the house now in front of him. Lightweight curtains allowed the image to project. The clear image of the outline of a woman.

The image of Birdsall flashed back through his eyes. "Oh God," said the killer. "Killed her. Lucille, baby," he reminisced. Eyes still fixed on the female form in front of him, his mind wandered. No sense of urgency within him to flee the scene. A psychopath stuck in the past, he recalled…

"You fix me a hamburger, baby?" he'd asked Birdsall as

she worked away in the kitchen of the Golden Pheasant. Methodically, she reached her hand into the hamburger, pulled it out, formed a ball, and splat it on the counter to make the patty.

He was turned on by this. He liked the force of her hand hitting the counter and the ooze of the meat under her palm. Everything she did turned him on. As Lucille squeezed the hamburger, he imagined her hands on him, kneading his back. "Uh huh," he sighed quietly as he watched her.

"What do you want on your burger?" she asked seriously, but with a gracious smile. Lucille was always gracious.

"Hmmm, can I have you?" he asked with a pure flirtatious grin. *Nice teeth,* thought Lucille. *Nice smile, too.*

"Nope, can't have me," she grinned, eyes dancing. She was now completely facing him, square on. "But you can have ketchup, mustard, butter, onions, lettuce, tomato an' pickle if you please."

Hard to believe she was the mother of a 5-year-old daughter, Betty Jane. As she stared at the stranger trying to seduce her, she thought about Betty Jane and the visit to see her child's father, Frank. This flirt in front of her was reminiscent of Frank. Bold, charismatic but potentially stubborn, just like her ex-husband.

Betty Jane stayed with her grandparents in Sturgeon Bay but Birdsall spent as much time with her as possible. Green Bay was only a forty-minute trip and she managed to have a normal relationship with Betty Jane.

Darling. No other way to describe the one gift Lucille would concede that Frank had given her. Spit curls framed her face. Slightly chubby legs and a giggle that could jump-start Lucille's distant stare into an immediate laugh.

Birdsall and Betty Jane had just visited Frank two days before. Jack drove the two of them. Betty Jane was a part of Lucille, therefore, Betty Jane became a focal point for Jack. He often looked at her and thought about the child he had lost as an infant along with his young wife many years before. Fatherhood had never revisited him, but through Betty Jane, he saw the child he never got to see grow.

Still smiling at the stranger who was still smiling at her and not saying a word, Lucille's mind continued to wander.

As Jack pulled up in front of Frank's place, he stopped the car, took both hands off the steering wheel and sucked her upper lip into his mouth. Then the bottom. "Uncle Jack is kissin' momma," giggled Betty Jane.

And then she was back.

"So, have you decided?" she asked the stranger once again.

She started to smell something and while trying to keep her gaze on the stranger, she turned her head to the right to catch sight of the grill. "Hold on!" she laughed. "All your fault. We've got fire." Lucille shoved two burned burgers off the grill.

"Fire all right," mumbled the stranger. "You are fire. Warm me," he whispered to himself, just out of earshot from Lucille.

He watched as she doused the grill. "Don't worry, I'm not going anywhere. Sit here all night if you want me too," said the stranger.

"That might not be good," flirted Birdsall. "I'm only allowed to burn I think, two burgers a night. With you I might burn more." She grinned.

His eyes never left her as he scanned her soft brown hair, pulled back and with a net around it. He pictured it tumbled out, running across him. Wild thoughts. He was completely infatuated with her.

She reached into the hamburger again, took out a ball and splat. "How do you like it, the burger that is?" asked Lucille.

"Not burned!" he laughed. "What is your name, doll?"

"Lucille, and I'm Jack's doll," she said.

"Who is Jack?" asked the stranger.

"He owns the place," answered Lucille.

"May own the place, but he doesn't own you. I don't see a ring on that pretty hand of yours, Lucille," said the stranger.

No longer fun.

His eyes lingered too long. *Wish Jack would get back soon,* thought Lucille.

"Make my burger how you think I would like it. I'm sure you can satisfy me just fine," said the stranger. A shiver crawled up Birdall's spine and the gracious smile left her lips. Game over. "Truly, how would you like your burger done sir?" she asked again.

"Sir? Awfully formal, Lucille doll," said the stranger.

Silence between them. He pushed forward and he could feel her pulling back. "Medium well please. Didn't mean to scare you. I think you're very pretty, that's all," he said to her. She worked at the grill, listening to the stranger but not facing him directly.

The front door of the house in front of the killer began to creak. He was jolted back to the present. Quick breath in and his pace hurried as he anticipated the opening of the door. Yep, the door was opening. His gait quickened into a walk-run as he made his way through early morning gray.

Gone and never to be found again. His job was done.

After he was about a hundred yards from the Golden Pheasant, he stopped. The dying brush along Willow Street was perfect. He walked off the road several feet and buried the hatchet in the dormant discolored weeds. Continuing his casual gait, he turned one last time, bloodied hands in his front pockets. Loved to dance, loved to see Lucille dance. His crazy eyes flickered as he reminisced again about the dance hall next to the bar. *Didn't have to be this way, Lucille. Didn't,* he thought to himself. Then the rage took hold again. Teeth began to grind. Then he swirled the spit in his mouth, gathered it into an angry ball, and sent it splat on the ground beneath him. "That's what you are now. Splat," he said of Jack and Lucille and walked away.

"Closed for Good"

No business would be done Monday at the Golden Pheasant, at least none legal.

Fred Van Beckum's pebbles thrown at the window would go unanswered. "Strange," he said aloud after casting the third stone.

"In those days, business was business and you stayed open all the time and worked it," said Fred's son, Norb.

At about 5 p.m. Monday, Mrs. William DeBroux, neighbor to the Golden Pheasant, was having a fit of curiosity. "Dad," she called out to her husband who had just returned home from work. "Dad," she called out again.

Irritated at being interrupted, Mr. DeBroux slowly walked into the kitchen. "What? Dinner ready yet?" he asked.

"No. Meatloaf is still cookin', but listen. There has not been any movement at the Pheasant all day and Jack's car is there. What do you make of that?" she asked.

DeBroux shrugged his shoulders, not thinking much of his wife's questions, which he saw as more gossip than anything else.

"What are you gonna do?" she asked him.

"What do you want me to do? Man's got a right to be closed for the day," he said.

"What if they're dead in there? I smelled something. What if they're asphyxiated in there? Go check," she pleaded.

DeBroux left out the back door and reluctantly approached the Pheasant. Jack's car was there alright. He began to smile. "Smart son-of-a-bitch. He's finally living life after all those years alone. I'll have to quiet the wife, make sure she leaves Jack and Lucille alone for their day of freedom," DeBroux said to himself.

"No gas smell honey. I'm sure they're fine. Lovers taking a day to themselves without the hustle of business," he said upon his return. His wife heard what he was saying but she did not truly listen.

Onions, beef, worcheshire sauce, bread and eggs — the smell of meatloaf filled the DeBroux home. She slowly opened the oven door and pulled the rack to check the loaf, not responding to her husband.

"Really, honey, nothing wrong there. Just two people taking time for something long overdue," he said, wrapping his arms gently around her back from behind.

Hope so, thought Mrs. DeBroux, still not saying anything. She had a sick feeling deep inside. She tried to put it out of her mind.

"Mom, I'm hungry," yelled the DeBrouxs' son, Martin, age 10. His hands and face were filthy with dirt. Martin was a rambunctious child. Brown hair and brown eyes and he seemed to make everything else brown! "Mr. Martin," said his mother. "Get in the bathroom and get washed up."

Martin slowly dragged his feet across the kitchen floor and down the short hallway to the bathroom. He lathered soap through his hands, dirty from playing marbles in the dirt all afternoon. Cat eye marbles were his favorite. He would play Jonathan for hours trying to win whatever he could. He was a good shot.

Martin approached his mom in the nightly routine. He smiled up at her. Momma's boy through and through. He held out his hands and turned them palms up. "Lookin' good Mr. Martin," smiled Mrs. DeBroux. "Take your place, sweetheart. I'll get the rest." Leaning down she whispered in his right ear: "You can have the end of the loaf along with your daddy." Martin grinned. He would do anything for his momma and she for him. He stuck a reddish cat's-eye marble in momma's apron as she walked away. He had never seen nor won a red one before.

That was the scene inside the Golden Pheasant, at least in John's room.

Red gush. A killer's trail led from the room to the back door.

Monday night arrived and left.

Mrs. DeBroux woke to find her bedspread balled up at the end of the bed. She pulled up the covers over her chest and that of her husband and tried again to get a good night's sleep.

At 4 a.m. she slowly opened her exhausted eyes for the third time. "Four a.m.," she muttered. She couldn't sleep. She got up and peered out the window at the Pheasant. She quickly inhaled as a shiver over took her once again.

"What is going on?" she whispered to herself. Milk warmed with honey joined her at the kitchen table. It was her soothing friend when she couldn't sleep.

Problem is, the only time she couldn't sleep was when something was truly wrong. Always like that from the time she was a little girl.

The early morning hours of Tuesday, May 20, 1930, would be no different.

She laid back down but awoke again at 5 a.m. "What's wrong, momma?" asked Martin who sleepily walked up to his mom, sitting at the kitchen table. She was already dressed and in her apron for breakfast.

"This is very nice, Martin," she said to him with the red cat's-eye marble in her right hand. She looked at it closely, like there was more to see. Inquisitive and so was Martin. "You little dickens, when did you put this in my apron Martin?" asked Mrs. DeBroux. "Last night momma, you like it?" asked Martin. "Yes honey, I do. Thoughtful boy," she said, hugging him.

"What are you thinkin' about momma?" asked Martin. She stared back, deep in thought, unable to shake her restless night of sleep.

Mrs. DeBroux would have done anything to keep her Martin safe, but that morning, curiosity grabbed her and in turn, she grabbed Martin.

"Martin, can you do momma a favor?" she asked with a hand on each of his shoulders.

"Sure momma, what is it?" he asked, grinning like the favorite child.

She walked him to the window and lifted him slightly so he could see the Golden Pheasant. "The blue streetcar there, Martin. I want you to climb up on it and look inside the Pheasant and then come back and tell me if you saw anything inside," said Mrs. DeBroux.

"But momma, you told me I can't go on there. Remember, Mr. Van Veghel gets mad when I get up there," said Martin, puzzled at his mother's suggestion.

"Just this one time Mr. Martin. It's like a mission and you like missions right Martin? You said you want to go into the Army and soldiers do missions. Can you be my little soldier this morning?" asked Mrs. DeBroux, smiling at young Martin.

"Yes ma'am!" he exclaimed.

"Shhhhh," Mrs. DeBroux quieted him. "This is between us. Now go get dressed for school, climb the street car and come back and momma will make you your favorite," said Mrs. DeBroux.

"Mashed potato pancakes?" giggled Martin.

"Yes, honey, from last night."

Martin scampered to his room. Right leg and then left leg into his jeans. He pulled on a blue-and-white striped shirt. White socks and blue sneakers snugged his feet.

And he was out the back door on a mission for momma.

He crept along, still worried about Mr. Van Veghel. He liked Mr. Van but he did not want to get in trouble. Martin approached the streetcar, which was used as a storehouse for the Pheasant and looked into John Van Veghel's bedroom.

His right foot hoisted him upward as he caught an out-side ridge of the car. Then his left leg on a middle ridge and finally the right leg made it's way to about a foot below the roof of the car.

Martin was out of breath, excited about his mission. He pulled himself up so his belly was on the roof of the car and his arms stretched outward in front of him, gripping the roof. At first he could not see in the bedroom window so he slithered his belly closer by pulling with his arms.

He lay there motionless for a few seconds, just like the people he saw inside.

Ten years old and he saw what no person should ever see in a lifetime, regardless of age. Certainly not at ten.

Martin shrieked with fear. "Momma, momma!" he shouted, still stuck on the roof of the streetcar and tears began streaming down his face.

Through the window he saw blood splattered everywhere and two people butchered like meat only half-prepared in a slaughterhouse. Birdsall's head was half hanging off the pillow, partially severed from repeated hacks with a hatchet. "Mr. Van" as Martin referred to him, was hardly recognizable, his dead eyes still staring at the ceiling as if still pleading for his life.

Martin didn't know exactly what he was looking at but he knew it was death and he was frightened. He continued to scream for help as he made his way off the streetcar and fell to the ground, his left leg caught underneath him. He scrambled to his feet. Crying uncontrollably he created a commotion along the way as he ran home.

Mrs. DeBroux moved for the door as she heard faint whimpers, her fingers playing nervously with the red marble in her right apron pocket. Then she realized it was her Martin's shrieks of horror. She flung open the door, just in time to catch a trembling Martin.

"Momma," he cried, burying himself in her belly.

"What is it Martin?" screamed Mrs. DeBroux, "What is it?"

"Momma," he tried again, snot running from his nose over his top lip and into his mouth, mixing with salty tears. "I can't breathe momma," he said and began to hyperventilate.

"Dad," called out Mrs. DeBroux to her husband. "Get in here right away!" she yelled to him again.

The young Martin could not stop shaking. And he could not stop crying. "It's bad, momma. There's blood, lots of blood. I think Mr. Van is dead," he choked out, refusing to let go of momma.

Frank Kupsack, Birdsall's ex-husband, woke early that morning as well. He was taking an early morning drag on a cigarette in his Milwaukee apartment. Ironically, he was thinking about Lucille that morning, but they weren't happy thoughts. He was thinking about all the times Lucille had sent telegrams from Sturgeon Bay telling him to hurry there

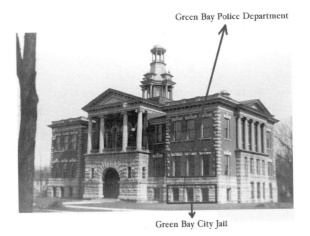

Green Bay Police Department

Green Bay City Jail

The original Green Bay City Hall, 300 N. Jefferson St., included the police department and city jail. Today, the parking lot of the current city hall is in its place. (Photo courtesy of Green Bay Police Department.)

because their baby, Betty Jane, was sick.

He wondered how he could be that naïve about Lucille over and over again. Still, each time he received a telegram about some emergency, he would go. Devoted to Lucille at one time and for always to his daughter. He had tried to send for Lucille and their baby many times but to no avail. He wanted custody of his daughter but he knew she was well-adjusted with her mother's care and the stability of her grandparents.

Kupsack took a slow long drag again on his cigarette, elbows propping him at the table. He stared straight ahead. He could almost see her angel face. Although they had not been good friends since the divorce, she was the mother of his child and for that he would always give her honor.

Time for work. He was a lathe installer and this time of year work was hectic, Sixteen hour days were the norm. He wondered what life would have been like had he been able to hold on to Lucille who simply was not happy. He thought about Uncle Jack, the man his young Betty Jane had described to her daddy as kissing his Lucille.

"So your momma has a new daddy for you, huh? Well, I am your daddy and no one else will ever be your daddy but me sweetheart," he told Betty Jane on a recent visit. Her curls and smile filled his mind as he readied himself for another day of labor. "Just wasn't meant to be," he said to himself. He put out his cigarette with his right hand and reached over with his left hand to pull on a work boot.

No. It was not. Not meant to be.

"The most grisly, brutal murders this area ever produced"
— **Deputy Chief Fred Matthews, Green Bay Police Department (Retired)**

"I need the sheriff here now," demanded Mrs. DeBroux as she called for help. Martin continued to tremble in her arms. Mrs. DeBroux cried as well. She knew by prompting of her son to check the Pheasant would leave a seared image of death imprinted in her son's mind. "Mr. Martin" would never be the same. Mrs. DeBroux would never quite forgive herself.

The commotion created by Martin's run home brought out the neighbors. One by one they began to gather at the Pheasant, even before deputies arrived on the scene.

The bodies were discovered at approximately 5:30 a.m. Tuesday morning and by 7 a.m. a crowd of more than 100 people had gathered.

Dozens of gawkers made their way through the roadhouse before police could contain the crime scene. "When grandpa got there, lots and lots of people were stripping souvenirs from inside. It was a crazy scene," said Norb Van Beckum.

"Ellen, grab that picture," said Mary as they moved through the roadhouse with an ever-flowing crowd. Hundreds, probably thousands of fingers were leaving prints all the while.

"Our family was mad at how it was handled. Everyone was fingerprinting everything, there was no control, " said Van Beckum.

The first deputies on scene attempted to take control. With a crowd looking on, they went through a second story window to gain entry. This opened into Birdsall's upstairs loft.

"Jesus," said one of the deputies as they squeezed through a narrow stairway, leading to Van Veghel's room, which had become a tomb of grisly brutality. "Oh, my God," said one of the deputies, staring at the mayhem in front of him. He closed his eyes briefly and then opened them again. Complete silence. Rooms where people sleep are quiet, but where they die it is silent.

"What kind of monster could do this?" he asked his partner, his eyes scanning the room. "Is this the most grotesque thing you have ever seen," replied the other, nearly gagging.

The unforgivable smell of death permeated the air. It's a difficult odor to describe, but impossible to forget.

Full rigor mortis had consumed both bodies. Head, neck, arms, hands, torso, legs, and feet were grotesquely stiff, all frozen in time. Lividity, the pooling of halted blood, gathered in and discolored their back sides. These natural occurrences helped establish time of death.

More deputies joined them and began to take inventory of the entire roadhouse. The bedroom adjoined the bar room. A trail of blood led from the room to the rear door.

"Hey, look at this," said one deputy, pointing to a dime slot machine on a stand near the bar. It had been smashed open.

Deputies in the basement discovered a quarter slot machine smashed and broken into as well. "Looks like this was broke open with a hatchet," said one of the deputies.

There had been a rash of slot machine-related burglaries in the area. Police suspected a slot machine theft ring was operating in the region but had few leads.

Police continued to comb through Van Veghel's bedroom for clues. A cash box in the bedroom filled with checks and currency was untouched. The cash register was closed with a $20 bill inside, but all silver was missing.

News of the hatchet killings traveled quickly. Van Veghel and Birdsall were well-liked in Titletown, Lucille maybe too well-liked thought some.

There was rumor that an unknown man had been frequenting the Golden Pheasant all spring and had tried to persuade Birdsall to go to Milwaukee with him. She had declined.

The crowd stayed together for hours, as if they were watching a movie, but this was real. Housewives made coffee and passed cups through the crowd along with bakery.

Dr. R.C. Buchanan made his way through the group. He was the first doctor called on scene. P.J. Gosin soon followed.

Buchanan, a man with 20 years experience, shrunk back in horror when he first saw the scene. "My dear God," he said methodically at first sight of John and Lucille. His right hand began to shake. He grabbed and covered it with his left in hopes that no one would notice.

He moved closer at the urging of deputies standing watch. First, he examined Van Veghel. "This is grotesque," he exclaimed. "Whoever did this crushed through his skull. The cuts are numerous and deep. Repeated slashing over and over with a sharp object."

"Lots of blunt trauma as well. Perhaps a handle was used. So deep are the wounds, they resemble the tearing discharge of a load of buckshot," said Buchanan, still visibly shaken.

Van Veghel's feet were on the floor and the rest of his body still covered by white bedding except for his head, which had become a mass of tissue with two pleading eyes staring up.

Buchanan moved back away from Van Veghel's body and shook his head at the deputy to his left.

"You have to find this madman. This is an animal of a person who did this. In all my career I have never seen anything so evil," said Buchanan.

Just then Dr. Gosin arrived on scene. Buchanan made his way around the foot of the bed and approached Birdsall.

"Look at this," said Buchanan, pointing to the woman's arms and the position of her body. "She fought, fought hard. Her arms are covered with deep slash marks. She awoke during the attack," said Buchanan, momentarily looking away. He knew Birdsall. He knew Van Veghel.

He lifted her stiffened left arm and showed Gosin how one slash went all the way to the bone. "Look at that face and neck. She never had a chance. All wounds are to the front. She never got a chance to turn and run," said Buchanan, again shaking his head.

Coroner Frank Hodek had requested the expertise of

both Buchanan and Gosin to complete the post mortem on the victims.

Flashbulbs sent light bouncing off the white walls. Photographs, from all angles, captured the scene. Once done, the room was examined for evidence. From the floor, walls, to ceiling, every corner was checked.

Buchannan, Gosin, and Hodek rolled the bodies from side to side and looked underneath. Limbs were forced into place before being zippered in the body bag. The sheets were collected and blood evidence was taken for typing and comparison, both intentionally and accidentally on the bottom of their shoes. Blood was everywhere.

Meanwhile outside, neighbors were biting into muffins, sipping coffee, and speculating on the meaning of the deaths.

Buchanan made a quick jerking motion forward and grabbed at his mouth after examining Birdsall, perhaps nearly vomiting at the sight of the hatchet murders. He waved off the offers of coffee and sweets as he exited the roadhouse.

Sheriff Nickolai was on the scene and Capt. Martin Burke of the Green Bay Police Department was questioning people in the neighborhood at the request of the Brown County Sheriff's Department.

"Sheriff's boy, Pete Van Veghel's kid," said Nickolai to Burke. Van Veghel had served as sheriff twice. "Unbelievable that this could happen to one of our own. How does something like this happen?" asked Nickolai.

Young Martin was at home resting under his mother's watch, while Mr. DeBroux mingled with the others outside.

"Looked like when grandpa kills chickens," cried Martin to his mother. "But it wasn't chickens, it was Mr. Van." The boy wept again, held by the arms of an exhausted mother.

Green Bay Detective Otto Cronce, a statewide fingerprint expert, was requested by the county and he arrived on scene shortly after 1 p.m. "This is chaos," exclaimed Cronce. He would later express frustration at not being allowed to work with the scene before it had been contaminated. He went through the motions and scattered black fingerprint dust throughout the scene. The metal bed posts were a perfect surface for prints. None were found.

That afternoon, deputies working in the basement found a lathe installer's hatchet with blood on it. This caused a swirl of activity. An attempt to locate request was sent out on Lucille's ex-husband, Kupsack, a lathe installer by trade in Milwaukee.

District Attorney Lewellen, Sheriff Nickolai and Coroner Hodek all took off together to an unnamed location at 1 p.m. creating much speculation.

Kupsack received a telegram Tuesday night informing him of the killing of Lucille. "No this has got to be a ploy to get me there. I'm sick of this," said Kupsack of his ex-wife's occasional exaggerated telegrams about the needs of their child. "Can't be," said Frank as he continued to question the telegram in front of him.

Kupsack was brought to Green Bay voluntarily at 8 a.m. Wednesday morning from Milwaukee. "I just want to clear my name," he told Sheriff Nickolai. "I don't blame you for suspecting me, especially after finding the hatchet, but my hatchet is home in my tool chest.

"Lucille and I were not the best of friends, but I would never hurt her. She is the mother of my child. I loved her," he said, still trying to convince police of his innocence. "I will cooperate in any way I can. I want you to catch whoever is responsible for the death of my child's mother," he continued, wiping nervous sweat from his forehead.

Kupsack was placed in the Brown County Jail but never charged. Irene Clowry, the other Pheasant waitress who last saw the victims alive, was asked to try to identify Kupsack. She recalled a couple of different men who had recently been in the Pheasant and talking to Lucille.

She could not identify Kupsack as one of those men.

The found hatchet was covered in chicken blood, not that of a person.

Kupsack was released from jail and went back to Milwaukee.

Clowny told authorities about a man who was kicked out of the Golden Pheasant late Sunday night by Van Veghel because he wouldn't leave Lucille alone. A friend of Van Veghel's drove the man home and during the drive it was rumored he kicked out one of the windows of the car.

"What are you going to do about this Jack? Bastard kicked out my window," said the friend to Van Veghel.

"Calm down," said Van Veghel. "I know him. He's good for it. I'll settle up with him tomorrow."

But tomorrow never arrived for Van Veghel, at least not in full light.

The former home of John (Jack) Van Veghel at 4259 Church Road in Bay Settlement, Wis. Van Veghel was one of two people murdered at the Golden Pheasant. (Photo by Mike R. Knetzger.)

An orchestra returning from a dance engagement in Antigo, reported to authorities they saw a large man making his way down Hwy. 78 on Monday morning between 5:30 and 6 a.m. This lead ran in the headlines of the *Green Bay Press-Gazette* for three days, before authorities finally conceded the man was likely a harmless vagrant with whom they were well familiar.

Two days later, on May 22, came another big lead. A blood-stained tablecloth was found in a barn near Elmore School. Police went rushing over only to find that the blood-stained tablecloth was a red figure on cloth. Another lead gone.

The murder weapon was never found. No one was ever charged in the case.

A positive — no burglaries or slot machine thefts were reported in the area for some time. If it was related, the bandits had left or decided to keep a low profile. If unrelated, would-be criminals were too afraid to be even remotely linked to such a hideous crime.

Jack Van Veghel loved to have family over to the Golden Pheasant for chicken and he often treated his nephews to nickel soda pop, recalled Norb Van Beckum. "Those were rough times. Everybody was poor," said Van Beckum. Summers were spent working on Aunt Ann Herman's farm (Jack's sister). Oats and wheat were staples.

"It was a different time," said Van Beckum. Certainly not a time when anyone would expect to be slaughtered. Family speculated that it had to be a slot machine burglary that had turned violent.

Still, authorities speculated that the murders could have happened early Monday morning and the separate crime of the slot machine burglary Monday night or early Tuesday morning. The theory held that thieves were attracted to the business Monday night because the building had been dark and without movement for several hours, presumably because

Van Veghel and Birdsall were already dead.

"Grandpa (Peter Van Veghel) said Uncle Jack must have known the killer, but many thought it might be someone from the insane asylum or poor farm in town that got loose," said Van Beckum.

Van Veghel attended St. Willebrord's for school so it was only fitting that the Catholic boy have his funeral there as well.

It was a cooler day with partial overcast.

And they began to arrive. Family, friends, and neighbors. It was the funeral of John (Jack) Van Veghel. All in black and dark clothing in contrast to the white and red he had been covered in at the time of his death.

They walked solemnly. This was not a life lived to its end. It was drastically cut short and at a time when Van Veghel seemed to have finally found love again after a decade of being a young widower.

Not fair. Not of this world.

"She was so shook up," said Van Beckum, referring to his grandmother, Henrietta (Nettie).

Everyone prayed and listened to the priest, he recalled. Grandma was crying as were others.

But to see Jack, they would be forced to look at the back of the church, explained Van Beckum. "His death was considered under suspicious circumstances so they would not allow the casket to be brought to the front of the church.

"Grandma was so upset, so were a lot of people," he continued. A brutal crime with a less than compassionate ending. Jack Van Veghel was a victim. Everyone seemed to be a suspect. And yet even at his death, Van Veghel himself was labeled suspect and left at the back of the church.

Strange Happenings

"You see that? That glass just toppled over," said Charles, a bartender at Lee's Cantonese, Green Bay. Strange occurrences had been happening on the property for decades. This was the original site of the Golden Pheasant, 2015 Willow Street, where Jack Van Veghel and Lucille Birdsall were murdered.

In 1974 the Don Quixote Supper Club was bought by Peter and Phillip Lee who turned it in to Lee's Cantonese.

A strip mall resides on the property now, at the northeast corner of University and Danz avenues.

Glasses were dancing on the bar and falling over. Charles reported hearing a woman talking on the telephone one night but the line was dead when he went to investigate. Believing the property was possibly haunted, the Lee brothers hired well-known local psychic, David Ray. Although he had conducted a séance in the past, it was not his forté. He accepted the work, he said, in an attempt to bring closure for the families of the victims and to bring understanding for the current property owners.

"Everything has alternate explanations," explained Ray. The séance was conducted in 1990 with approximately thirteen people present including descendants of the victims. Ray served as a "channel," which brings contact between a spirit and a person here.

It was a stormy night, sixty years after Birdsall and Van Veghel had been chopped to death. And on that night in 1990, Lucille came to the group.

All the participants sat in the dining room together with hands lightly touching. A quiet came over the group with only red light piercing through the darkness. The lighting was for technical reasons but eerily connected to the bloody destiny of the victims.

"We're here to try to get more information on this case and see if we can reach the victims," instructed Ray.

He employed a technique known as "automatic writing." With eyes closed, the channel, also known as a medium, holds a pen on a piece of paper.

When it began, Birdsall talked for the first time in 60

years through the writing technique. Contrary to physical evidence, she told the group that Van Veghel had been awakened by the killer.

"He had to be gotten out of the way first," she said through Ray. She went on to explain in a very slow process of the pen moving across the paper, that she had met her killer some days before. She said he was interested in her and she told him about Van Veghel, which had angered him.

"Itinerant farm laborer" scrolled across the paper.

"There was one thing I didn't like," said Ray. "She said his name was Jack."

Confusing.

"I asked people to come up with questions they wanted to ask. Someone asked what kind of weapon was used," said Ray.

The words "corn knife" scrolled across the paper once again. "It was very difficult to read," said Ray.

A knocking noise began to rivet the room. A hush fell over the participants. Then they began again in the depth of red tones.

"We asked Lucille what else she could tell us," said Ray. Very clearly the auto-writing continued. She said the knife was unwrapped and taken out of a gunny sack.

Birdsall was asked by one member of the group whether a hatchet found buried in the yard was the weapon and her answer was no. She said it was probably just from the kitchen.

The group became more and more bold. The rain continued to pour and so did the questions, said Ray.

Materialization is having a spirit take a physical form. Lucille and/or Jack were asked if they could project an image of their killer.

"One of the women said she could see him. He was profiled and had a dark beard with a prominent nose," said Ray.

Hands still touching and a tension in the room. Ray asked Birdsall or Van Veghel to tell them the location of the killer. "He's dead," flowed the pen on the paper. Ray said the killer died between 1940 and 1942 in a highway accident coming from Chicago.

Ray said it's not unusual for many to doubt the validity of séance paranormal events. "Someone at the table asked if there was any other evidence of spirit contact," he explained. He brought out a padlock, locked it in front of the group and placed it on the table in front of everyone.

"Can anyone here open the lock?" he asked of all spirits present.

In front of everyone, the lock, it unlocked, Ray said,

Birdsall told the group she had told her killer about Van Veghel in an effort to get rid of the man.

"We got raps. You ask if the spirits can "rap out" messages," explained Ray.

One rap means yes, two means no.

Did Birdsall know her killer?

"Rap."

The silence in the red-glowing room was deafening.

"Sheriff Told Man Admitted Killing Couple" — *Green Bay Press-Gazette, Sept. 30, 1930*

"He said she was his girl, his baby," said Bernard Coy to his cellmate by fate, W. G. Foss.

Foss had been picked up in Sturgeon Bay and was being held there for Sheboygan authorities.

It was after 10 p.m. and both men were bored and restless. Foss had been on the run for weeks and had not had the love of a woman in quite some time.

His mind wandered as Coy spoke of the woman his friend, Thomas Donnelly, claimed was his girlfriend. Her name was Lucille Birdsall. She was beautiful. She was dead. Still, Foss enjoyed hearing about her because she was a woman and he liked having a woman on his mind.

"Tell me more," said Foss with a dirty chuckle. "What else he tell you about her?"

"She kissed like an angel," said Coy. "She could cook anything, satisfy a man real well," said Coy, who was on the bottom bunk and Foss on the top.

Miserable, the two escaped their discomfort with exchanged fantasy, although Coy insisted to Foss that the fantasy of Donnelly killing his love and her lover was indeed real.

Bang. Bang. A knocking sound from the adjoining cell threatened their sanity. Stuck in a 7 by 7 box of gray concrete, Coy was stretched out on his bunk and rolled to his right side. He hung off the side and peered at Foss who was visibly annoyed.

"Shut up," called out Foss to the phantom knock, his voice echoing off the walls. "Tell me more Bernie, more about this Donnelly," said Foss.

"Well, he had this girl named Lucille. Saw her often at a place in Green Bay called the Pheasant," whispered Coy.

"Go on," prodded Foss. Bang. Bang. Bang. The annoying knocks continued. "Enough," yelled Foss. "Knock it off or I'll bust your head first chance," bellowed Foss again.

The jailer came out. "What's going on boys?" he asked.

Foss knew better than to answer. He had been in jail before. Coy, too. This was just a brief stop for both. No need to get more added time for being disorderly.

"So, what's the problem?" asked the jailer again. Stern look. Still silence. "I don't want to hear anymore out of either one of you for the rest of the night," he said and walked away, done with his rounds for the night.

Coy and Foss burst out laughing. Foss buried his head in his pillow, a mass of belly rollin' as the two giggled like school boys talking about girls. But they weren't talking about girls. They were talking about the hacking to death of a 24-year-old mother of one and her widower boyfriend.

Coy loved to tell a good story. He was the ultimate male gossiper. "I'm tellin' you Foss, he did it. Donnelly, he's famous. He's the hatchet murderer in Titletown."

Picked up in Sturgeon Bay for Sheboygan authorities, Coy had Green Bay ties and had lived there. He knew the Golden Pheasant. He also knew Happy Hanson's, a brothel down the street. Knew them both well.

Soda parlors, chicken dinners and fishing on the Fox River. That was Coy's scene. That and talking. Never stopped. He made friends easily and enemies just as well because of his free mouth. Intelligent in thought but an imbecile at times in action. Never knew when to stop.

"He told me he did it. Told me plain as this cell," said Coy again to Foss.

Interesting man, thought Foss. "Amazing how he got away with it," he said to Coy. "Did he tell you why?"

"Yep," said Coy. "Ain't nobody taking Thomas Donnelly's girl. Nobody."

"But are you sure this Lucille was his girl?" asked Foss. "Seems to me she was with someone else. Sounds like this Donnelly thought of her as his girl but she really wasn't."

"Don't know. All I know is what he told me and he told me he used a hatchet," said Coy. "First to take out the man who took his girl. Second to make her pay. But I think he regretted it from how he talked about her."

"Regretted how?"

"Called her angel. Said he killed his angel," explained Coy, starting to tire of delving into the details.

"We were laying there and he started screamin'," reenacted Coy.

"What?" whispered Foss, looking up where Coy was hanging off his bunk again. Coy silently started to fling his bunk blanket all over the bed and contort his face into painful expressions.

"What the hell?" whispered Foss, ducking out of the way. "Are you nuts or what?"

Coy continued to bounce the bunk and make quiet squeals. Finally he stopped and laid down, stretched out quietly on the bunk once again.

"You done, you crazy bastard?" whispered Foss. "What was that all about?"

"I told you," said Coy. "Donnelly regretted it. He had nightmares when I was with him. He would wake up angry yelling out 'angel.' Other cellmates, they thought he was calling for someone to rescue him from jail. He wanted them to think that. Me, he told the truth. He was cryin'. Said he killed his angel. When I asked what angel, he said her name. Told me all about Lucille."

Foss was starting to believe. Why would Bernie lie to him? No point. Crazy or not, he was convincing and he knew details.

Eventually authorities retrieved Foss from Sturgeon Bay and he was transported to the Sheboygan County Jail.

Pure coincidence. Maybe fate.

Foss was placed in a cell next to that of Thomas Donnelly. Donnelly was also known under the alias name of Jim McGilth. He was in the Sheboygan jail on drunk and disorderly charges.

Nervous though. Too nervous and anxious to get out for a man soon to be released on minor charges, thought Foss.

The two began to talk. Foss knew Donnelly, but Donnelly did not know Foss.

One night Foss heard some whimpering, followed by an angry plead of "angel". He was barely awake at the time, but the commotion next to him sent chills through his mind.

Wow,, thought Foss. *I do have a killer in the cell next to me. That Coy was right!,*

Morning came. Breakfast was slid through the bars. The two ate. Foss ever so slowly struck up a conversation. "Sleep good?" he asked the exhausted looking Donnelly.

"Why the hell you ask?" asked Donnelly.

"Just wondering," said Foss.

Donnelly threw his tray across the cell, slamming it against the wall and bread flying. Anger. Pure anger on his face. He stared at Foss, who played dumb.

"What's wrong? You not hungry?" asked Foss.

"Listen, you want to get out of here, together?"

"What you mean?"

"I have to get out of here and soon."

"But you will be out of here soon," said Foss.

"Not soon enough," said Donnelly through clenched teeth. He leaned forward, sitting with an elbow on each knee. Left hand under his chin, contemplating the future. Right hand pressing in on his forehead, right above his brow, where a headache had begun to throb.

"There's a murder rap hanging over me at Green Bay," Donnelly said.

"Murder?

"Yep, murder."

Foss was impressed by Donnelly. Indeed, it appeared Coy was right. Although Donnelly never spoke in detail to Foss about the double hatchet murder in Green Bay, he indicated he was in trouble. Big trouble. And it was for murder.

The two befriended each other and spent the next two weeks trying to escape the Sheboygan jail. It would not be. Authorities foiled the attempt. Foss, only thinking of himself, explained to authorities that it was Donnelly's plan because he was facing a murder rap in Green Bay.

Brown County Sheriff Nickolai was notified by Sheboygan authorities. He traveled to Sheboygan to meet with Donnelly.

Donnelly denied discussing the murder, as did Bernard Coy. That left Foss a questionable witness.

"Yes, I was in your city at the time of the murders," admitted a composed Donnelly as the sheriff questioned him. "That doesn't mean I did it. Never said I did it," quipped Donnelly.

"Come on Donnelly. I have information otherwise. Remember Bernie Coy? He says you did it," fired Sheriff Nickolai.

Donnelly sat quiet but still composed. Nickolai could feel rage slowly building in Donnelly. He motioned for another jailer to join him. He did the questioning himself. No investigator. This was the biggest crime of the century. It had happened in his jurisdiction. He would squeeze a confession out of Donnelly. He believed with all that was within him that Donnelly could be their man.

But he had no weapon. Conflicting motives. No proof that Donnelly and Lucille Birdsall had ever met. Green Bay Det. Martin Burke, even with his skill, could locate no witnesses who had seen the two together. Waitress Irene Clowry couldn't even confirm seeing Donnelly.

"All right Donnelly, let's try this again. Your cell "neighbor" Foss says you did it. Says you call out for your *angel*, Lucille Birdsall, during night terrors. Says you told him you needed out of here because we were coming for you in Green Bay on charges of murder. Double murder," said the sheriff.

"Son-of-a-bitch. That double-crossing rat," hollered Donnelly.

Donnelly cursed Foss up and down. Sheriff Nickolai listened carefully for anything that would directly incriminate Donnelly. He didn't need much. Just enough to hold him on suspicion. Visibly distraught, Donnelly continued to cuss but never accused Foss of trying to frame him.

If he were clearly innocent, thought Nickolai, he would have accused him of a framing. He did not. Nothing in the case was clear, other than the butchering of two people.

He left without enough to hold Donnelly.

Donnelly left for Milwaukee after his time in Sheboygan was served.

Coy continued to spend some time in Green Bay but eventually moved.

Foss never recanted his claims.

An inquest into the murders was held in the fall of 1930 but gleaned no new information.

The double hatchet murder continued to make headlines for years after, not because of progress but because a grisly crime had gone unpunished. A young Martin lived with the image of death in his mind.

A 5-year-old girl would grow up without her mother. A widowed businessman would die a brutal death without ever being afforded the chance to raise a family.

Two families would live forever without Jack Van Veghel and Lucille Birdsall. Seventy-five years later it's still the cold case of all cold cases in Titletown. For a place known as the Frigid Tundra, this crime also compliments that name but in a grotesque way.

Somebody did it.

"5 Wounded in Bank Holdup" — Green Bay Press-Gazette, July 20, 1931.

SOUTH SIDE STATE BANK ROBBERY

July 19, 1931 — Somewhere in St. Paul, Minnesota:

"Listen, tomorrow we head for Green Bay, we will be in and out of the bank before that small town even knows what hit 'em. If anyone gets in our way, you know what to do," he said looking down the barrel of his 50-round Tommy Sub Machine gun and snickering along with his fellow gangsters.

July 20, 1931 — Green Bay, Wisconsin:

"Extra! Extra! Read all about it!" would soon be the paperboy's caw as headline news was a few hours from now. The 700 block of South Broadway on the City's west side was a center for business and pleasure. This Monday in Green Bay, Wis., would be a day that forever impacted the lives of many and permanently changed it for a few.

It was 10 a.m. on this beautiful summer day and temperatures would soon reach 90 degrees. The cloud cover from the much-needed rains the night before would give way to the sunshine and heat. A simple act of opening windows turned on "air conditioners," which wouldn't offer much relief from the high humidity provided by the waters of the Fox River a couple of hundred feet to the east of Broadway.

With W. Mason Street (State Highway 54) to the north and Third Street to the south, this high traffic area was a perfect location for business and industry. Running east and west, the W. Mason Street bridge carried the common 1930's Chevrolet Coach and Model-T Ford over the Fox River to the east side. Parallel to the south of E. Mason Street, Third Street ended at the Fox River and led west into the neighborhood towards S. Ashland Avenue (State Highway 32), a primary north-south thoroughfare. Residents and visitors alike frequented Schefe's Meat Market, Tickler's Hardware Store, Belleau's Drug Store, Geo. Buck's Grocery Store, Gilmore and Erdmann's Barbershops, and the South Side Clothing Company, just to name a few. Some would just stop underneath the awning's shade to catch a break from the heat. These storefronts would soon become the concrete bunkers customers would hide behind.

Mid-block at 708-710 S. Broadway, along the west side of the street, stood the South Side State Bank. The bank occupied the lower level of this two-story, eye catching architectural structure. The ornamental gray concrete and stone with its inset windows created a ledge that often served as a chair for guys having a smoke or watching for their future wives as the well-dressed ladies walked by. The entrance to the bank was in the middle of the building and ornamental vertical pillars outlined the doorway.

A famous gangster's girlfriend would frequent the "high-class" Red Black's tavern directly to the north of the bank. Customers in a hurry would park in the alley to the south for a quick transaction and then leave toward the back alley.

Above the bank, physician Paul M. Clifford would treat the common ailments of the day while dentist Raphael E. O'Shea removed a tooth or two with little anesthesia and lots of pain. Western Refrigerator Line did its best to help keep food cool and ladies inside the South Side Beauty Shop would soon be in for a "hair-raising" experience.

Slate gray and similar hues of brick and concrete were across the street from the bank. These two-story buildings

were built with the architects' care. The common contrast-
ing brick arch above each window and the chiseled name
plate near the roofline made them unique. An outstretched
awning meant business was open for the day. A music store,
two barbers and a printing office were directly across from
the bank. A hundred feet to the north near W. Mason Street,
Buck's grocery would be just close enough to watch a gun
battle. Just to the south was a café and patrons inside would
soon see bullets coming their way.

Vehicles lined both sides of the street making a parking
space hard to come by. The more common V-6 Chevrolet
Coach had outsold the smaller 4-cylinder Ford. Chevrolet's
reign would last only six more months, but their dark gray or
black cars dominated the stalls this day. Henry Huth's Soft
Drink delivery truck would take up a few parking spaces just
to the north of the bank.

The tree-lined sidewalks played host to the masses where
young and old alike would pass by or chat for the day. The
recession was on the minds of all, but hope could be found
in the Star Spangled Banner, which had been signed into law
in March. Then on May 1 the world's tallest building was
built, the Empire State Building. These were icons of hope,
but the locals would often talk about what was to become
a storybook team. Their beloved Green Bay Packers had
just won their second straight championship the previous
year and the regular season was only two months away. The
players played for the love of the sport. The fans followed to
cheer them on and help forget, for a brief moment, how they
were going to make ends meet from one week to the next.
Although an adult beverage or two may also help one cope,
The Volstead Act - Prohibition (the 18th Amendment) made
that illegal but not completely unavailable.

Inside the police department at 122 N. Jefferson Street on
the City's east side, a fit 65-year-old Chief Thomas E. Hawley
had reviewed the arrests from the weekend along with the

police reports to go along with them. Some of the locked up vagrants, in the city jail below, could sometimes be heard talking as they waited their turn in front of the bench. Laying on the "planks" or peering in between the jail bars at the well-kept lawn and tree-lined street they would contemplate their fate. Would it be banishment from the city? Some hard time in Wisconsin's first workhouse? In the July heat, banishment was the vagrant's preference, but often contrary to the judge's desire. Convictions were the norm, appeals were uncommon and justice was swift with cases being disposed within 24 to 72 hours of arrest. The wheels of justice were smooth.

Forty-five-year-old Lieutenant Detective August "Gus" Delloye, a police gun battle veteran from a few years prior, and Captain Martin Burke, second in command, were reviewing their cases and every so often chatting with the chief. A true leader of this 35-man department, Chief Hawley was a great listener and forward thinker. He would always lend an ear to Delloye and Burke as they wondered aloud when the police radio would find its way into Green Bay. Chief Hawley was also awaiting Common Council approval to pay for portable police radios in four squad cars. The police call box was archaic and didn't allow for quick information relay. With crimes in progress, the needed information would often come too late. This worked to the criminals' advantage and helped facilitate escape.

Chief Hawley, a thin, short, quiet man who was once told that he was a bit light and couldn't be a cop, had been in charge of the police department for the past 34 years. He understood the dynamic nature of his position. Leading the troops or disciplining them fairly when needed, hiring and firing, preparing budgets, acquiring equipment, planning for the future, and convincing the city council to give him the funds to make it all happen. Six months earlier, he convinced the council to temporarily fund four additional motorcycle officers. These new officers helped expand police service to

The shot-up squad car in which the officers were riding. (Photo courtesy of the Green Bay Press-Gazette.)

the hardworking middle class citizens living in the outskirts. He would be speaking in front of the council again later this month to justify the continued funding. If denied, he would have to lay them off, which he didn't want to do. An event, any event, to justify these positions would help make the case. Chief Hawley understood the crime rate game. If crime is up, he needed more officers. If crime was down, his agency was doing a great job.

In contrast, Hawley could also use a year of little notoriety. The previous three years had been rough. In 1928, Delloye, one of his finest detectives, had been seriously wounded in a gun battle with fellow officers in a sad case of mistaken identity and questionable police work. The next year, a handful of citizens accused Chief Hawley of failing to enforce Prohibition and called for his job. The police and fire commission disagreed and Hawley remained at his post. Then, his agency's resources were tasked again in 1930, assisting the county sheriff with the grizzly and gory investigation of the region's most horrifying double murder at a roadhouse known as the Golden Pheasant. The victims were hacked to death and their killer was still at large.

Lieutenant Detective Delloye, affectionately called "Gus," was the son of a Belgian born immigrant who loved his job. This former Chicago firefighter was tri-lingual. He spoke and wrote English, Belgium, and French. His type "A" personality drove him and he was not one to give up. He poured his heart and soul into his work and family life. He had never been reprimanded and was the recipient of numerous citations for valor. From 1916 thru 1926, he never missed a day of work to sickness, nor did he take a vacation day. Standing a about 5 ft. 7 inches tall and naturally strong, his chiseled chin, round babyfaced cheeks, brown piercing eyes, and handsome dark hair, commanded attention and the badge demanded respect. Delloye fit the profile, a competent cop, who served his city well. He enjoyed the pursuit, the investigation, solving the case, and bringing men to justice. He was full of life, loved it, and appreciated it; a few years prior, extortionists almost took it. Warriors often say, "A man doesn't know what it's like to live until he's almost died." Delloye knew what that meant.

Police work is stressful and laughter is the best medicine. Like most cops, Delloye had a unique and necessary sense of humor. In his later years, once all the "principals were dead," he would often tell one of his funnier stories.

It was in the early 1920's. Delloye only had a few years on and was walking his Main Street beat. It was about 2 a.m. He knew what was "normal" and noticed the slightest thing out of place. He shined his flashlight in each doorway while passing by. It allowed him to peer inside and make sure all was well. Suddenly, his flashlight illuminated a figure. A man faced him through a glass door. He had a gun in his right hand. Startled, Delloye jumped back, drew his weapon, pulled the trigger, and two rounds passed through the window and into its target. But the man didn't fall. *What the hell?* Delloye thought to himself. He looked closer and then realized he had done a fine job destroying a mannequin. A weapon it wasn't holding, but rather a cigar. Realizing his mistake, the officer "fanned ass" and never told a soul. The next day, detectives investigated and never found out who did it.

Delloye' good friend and colleague, Capt. Burke, shared a similar drive and led by example. The true qualities of a leader: hard work, integrity, dedication to service, justice and the American way, Capt. Burke wouldn't settle for anything less. A round, frameless, gold eyepiece with a lapel cord was the only thing missing from his attire. Add that and President Roosevelt would have been jealous. Burke's tall, but thin stature looked down on the average man. His well-trimmed mustache followed his upper lip and supported his long nose. An inquisitive look came natural to him and the above-the-collar cut, brown and combed to the right, rounded off his leader look.

Burke was a walking records department. His signature black-colored vest with six outside front pockets, three on each side, were filled with index cards. Each card contained the names, descriptions, and records of known local criminals. Officers often consulted Burke or reached into his vest to run a records check. If the name wasn't found then the offender didn't have a criminal history. A bit archaic, but it worked. Burke and Delloye shared this information and knew the criminal element well.

Officer Elmer DeNamur was a patrol officer and the department mechanic in charge of the "fleet," which consisted of three squad cars and a few motorcycles. The primary patrol car, a 1931 Chevrolet Coach with a hardworking V-8 under the hood, was new this year and waiting in the parking lot for its next call for service. Most of the time, this police department of 36 sworn officers were on foot patrol and responded to their call box for the next order of business. Response times were completely dependent on how far the foot patrol officer was from his box. If unheard, no one else could open the locked box and the call may be left unanswered for several minutes. However, if it was an emergency, the motor officers could also respond from the police department. All call boxes would be activated throughout the entire city alerting foot patrol officers simultaneously. 911 was unheard of and the phone number to the police department was "Adams 87," which was difficult to remember and dial under the stress of an emergency...

Inside the South Side State Bank

"Hey, Bernice only one hour until lunch time...you wanna stop at Red Blacks for lunch?" assistant cashier Frank Slupinski asked teller Bernice "Bea" Sager. Frank was behind the cage and resting his arms on the marble countertop. He was exhausted from another night of interrupted sleep. Baby Jean, his newborn daughter of exactly 30 days, had woken twice during the night. Frank's mind drifted to thoughts of

The scene outside the bank shortly after bandits, armed with Tommy guns, seriously wounded Det. August Delloye and fled. (Photo courtesy of the Green Bay Press-Gazette.)

his wife Julia. He liked to have her at home, but missed the days working together at the West Side Bank.

"Sure," replied Sager, startlling Frank back into an upright position. "Maybe we will run into Dillinger's girl, Evelyn Frechette. She hangs out there!" she said jokingly.

Overhearing their conversation, teller Earl Cayer quipped, "That gossip has yet to be confirmed."

Teller William Golden was helping customer H.C. Erbe while thirteen-year-old Geraldine Miller waited in line. "I tell ya, Mr. Erbe," said Golden, "rumor has it that Dillinger, thankfully, is in prison for the time being. The less reason he has to come here the better."

"Dillinger, come to Green Bay, yeah right!" said savings teller Norbert Allen walking past Golden on his way to the main office.

These were words they would all soon regret.

"Alright, it's 11:00 a.m., we are right on schedule…We're almost there, just relax…take a swig of this, it will help take the edge off!" one gangster confidently mentioned to another as they turned right from W. Mason Street and headed south towards the South Side State Bank.

"Are they still behind us? Are they still behind us?" the driver wondered aloud inquiring about the other carload of gangsters following close behind.

"Yes, yes, right behind us…" in their black Pierce Arrow or Auburn, a likely choice for gangsters who were among the few that could afford it and, if not, steal it. The vehicle drove slowly past the bank; turned right on Third Street and stopped. These two gangsters would soon witness their plans interrupted.

Locked and loaded and ready to "rock-n-roll" with their fully automatic .45-caliber Tommy sub machine guns concealed underneath their three-piece suits, they didn't expect much resistance. Their stylish midnight blue or dark gray double-breasted suits with squared shoulders supported the sheer power of the Tommy gun; enough to give even the worst gangster confidence. Their sharp dress would help maintain the element of surprise.

They could easily be taken for a businessman wishing to make a transaction or open an account. Unmasked, with one wearing a straw hat, these "Italian looking" gangsters prepared for their quick take and robbery of the South Side State Bank. Well planned and experienced, it was now time to execute the mission.

The second vehicle, a gangsters' special, the 1930's dark blue or black Nash, rolled up and stopped at the bank's front doors. The Nash was very roomy allowing generous head and legroom. Gangsters made maximum use of this space and mounted a tripod or turret on the floor for their Tommy gun, which provided 360-degree firepower. Gangsters also creatively used the dashboard for their Tommy gun. A swivel bracket mounted on the dash worked well for spraying .45-caliber rounds forward and from side to side.

Three gangsters exited the Nash and entered the bank while two others remained out front; one on the sidewalk and the other in the vehicle, both with Tommy guns. It was evident to any passers-by that a robbery was in progress. It was anticipated that this show of force would prevent any armed vigilante resistance.

Inside the print shop across the street, A.W. Juster stood, frozen for a brief second, while he watched the three gun-men hurry into the bank. Juster ran to the phone and called police.

"Everybody, get your hands up! Get in the corner! Get in the corner! On the floor or we will blow your damn heads off!" the gangsters yelled with their Tommy guns and revolvers pointed at the terrified employees and customers.

Those who didn't listen were shoved violently into a corner. Two gangsters jumped over the cashier's desk, behind the cash cages, and began empting the drawers. Another remained near the door. He appeared to be the leader, commanding most of the movements, and covering the terrified employees and customers with his machine gun in hand.

One gunman demanded Slupinski open the vault and he complied. Slupinski was then ordered to the floor and the gangsters began clearing out the vault.

Slupinski saw Julia cradling Jean in her arms. "Oh, God," he thought to himself, closing his eyes. Not enough time lately with his beautiful Julia. Accustomed to breakfast every morning from his doting wife, the last month had been a change in routine since the much anticipated birth of Jean.

He had dined on fried eggs and buttered white toast at Brehme's diner down the street. Slupinski could still see Julia's blue eyes smiling at him at the door of their two-bedroom apartment on Hubbard Street. He felt pure fear. "We have a baby, Lord. Please bring me home to them." He prayed to himself and felt a rough arm plow into his back.

He could see the gangster's feet shuffling from side to side as he cleared the shelves. Fearing death, Slupinski's mind didn't focus much on the gangster's description, but noted, briefly, that he was 30 to 35 years old and appeared Italian.

Unfortunately, the gangsters didn't find much in the vault. About $7,000 in hand was an inadequate payout for this risky business.

"Where are the securities and gold? Where are they?" they demanded from Slupinski while at the same time kicking and slugging him.

Slupinski flashed to Julia again. He could see the white velvet dress she wore on their wedding day. He could feel the giggle in her voice the day she thanked him for red roses. She was suffering ankle pain and the flowers were the beginning of their banking courtship.

Fearful for his life, Slupinski honestly and nervously answered, "I swear there is no more I can get to...the cashier has the keys!"

"You liar!" the gangster yelled and repeatedly clubbed Slupinski with the wooden butt of the Tommy gun, crushing his nose and deviating his septum, crushing cheekbones, and lacerating his face. Slupinski moaned aloud as he slipped into unconsciousness, bleeding profusely.

Working as a bank teller was a risk. It was a risk Slupinski knew well. He was glad his wife was out of the bank. She enjoyed the customers, working with the safe deposit boxes and Christmas club accounts. Customers on occasion brought her candy. Slupinski was serious and quiet, but he had Julia and he also shared in the candy.

Seventy dollars a month as a teller — hardly worth a man's life. "He could talk a lot," Slupinski's wife would later recall. "They never had beating and robbing in broad daylight like that."

Slupinski was lying in a quickly forming pool of blood. Julia, unaware of her husband's fate, was trying to keep the baby cool in the apartment. "It was so hot, the walls of our apartment were sweating," Julia, now age 102, explained.

Cayer made the mistake of agreeing with Slupinski and was similarly beat until he too fell unconscious bleeding from the head and face next to Sager.

Spatters of blood tattooed her blouse. Cayer's limp body touched hers and blood oozed from his head. "Stop it! Stop it!" Sager screamed at the gangsters while doing her best to calm the terrified 13-year-old, now in tears.

Oblivious to what was going on inside the bank, middle-aged customer Wilfred Stram leisurely walked in to complete a transaction. "Stick 'em up!" the armed bandit ordered Stram.

Startled and without thought, his hands flew up in the air while staring down the gun barrel. "Get down on the ground with the others," demanded the gangster. Stram willingly complied. He would later tell his account again and again to curious bystanders, who, in a strange way, wished they had been there.

"BRRING, BRRING" the phone inside the bank rang twice. All became silent for a moment except for some faint fearful whimpers. "You! You! Get over here," said one of the gangsters while pointing his Tommy gun at Allen. He nervously and slowly walked towards the heavily armed gangster thinking, "I always wanted to be a priest. Now I wish I had been."

The gangster nudged him forward, "You answer the phone and make like there is nothing wrong. No foolin! You understand?" The anxiety could be heard in the gangster's voice. With the barrel now pressed against his side, the message was clear, comply or die. "No sir, Mr. Van Vonderen is not in…" said Allen to the caller. Just then, "We've got company boys…" said one of the gangsters.

At the Police Department

"Police department, Patton," the gruff veteran Sergeant answered the phone.

"You better send someone, the South Side State Bank is being robbed!" reported A.W. Juster inside the Commercial Printing office across the street from the bank.

"We are on our way!"

Just as he hung up another call came in, "The South Side State Bank has just *been* robbed!" reported a dentist whose office was above the bank.

"Hey chief, we've gotten some calls that the South Side State Bank has just been robbed…" the sergeant told Hawley.

"Delloye, Burke, DaNamur, let's go, the South Side State Bank has just been robbed!" the chief shouted while preparing to leave himself. Patton stood up to leave, but Hawley stopped him.

"Patton, stay here, man the phones. *Do not* sound the

general alarm to all those call boxes until we are at least half way there. If they're still around, they are going to hear the alarm and take off." Unlike many leaders, Hawley never forgot where he came from and insisted on going on any potentially dangerous call. It was yet another reason that his officers respected him.

Hawley hurried into the garage and grabbed a shotgun. He chambered a round. Bam! Buck shot pelted the ceiling. In his haste, he accidentally had his finger on the trigger and fired off a round. Startled, amazed and laughing. Hawley made his way outside.

Everybody climbed into one squad car, a Chevy coach, parked outside. Officer DeNamur drove and Det. Delloye sat next to him. In the back behind DeNamur sat Chief Hawley and to his right Det. Burke. The Chief joked, "Hey Delloye, it's your turn this week, stick your head out the window and be the siren."

Believing the robbery was over, DeNamur parked the squad car at an angle by the southeast corner of the building, onto the sidewalk, and partially facing the south alley.

"Shit, the cops!" shouted one of the gangsters inside the Nash. He squeezed the trigger of the Tommy gun unloading fifty .45 caliber rounds in four to seven seconds.

"What the hell is going on?" screamed Hawley as the squad windows began to shatter and the street erupted in gunfire. The well-trained and experienced gangster inside the Nash crushed the trigger of his Tommy gun and filled the squad with lead. DeNamur had inadvertently parked directly in front of the gangsters' Nash that was still in front of the bank. This was tactical mistake that would forever haunt Hawley.

He would later tell the media, "Our tactics would have been different had it been known that the robbers were still at work. We left with the understanding that the hold-up had been committed and the robbers had left. Ninety-nine times out of a hundred by the time anyone can call in, and the squad car can reach the bank, the robbers have left."

Like a colony of frenzied ants, frightened people scattered in all directions. Parents grabbed their children and ran, colliding with each other, stumbling, and falling, whatever it took to get away. Cowering behind doors, trees, and automobiles or hiding in garbage cans — anything would become cover in this deadly game of hide-and-seek. Their high-pitched screams were muffled by the automatic gunfire. Traffic in both directions stalled.

"Where the hell is that coming from?" Delloye immediately thought to himself upon hearing the bark of a Tommy submachine gun over his right shoulder. He looked in the same direction and saw the fire-breathing barrel of the Tommy gun spitting .45-caliber rounds, shattering the squad windows and slicing through the metal body like butter.

Something struck his left eye, probably a ricochet round or a shard of glass, but his adrenaline temporarily masked the pain. "Get to cover, get to cover!" Delloye thought to himself as he opened the passenger side door and stood up less than ten feet from the automatic machine gun.

Instinctively, Delloye turned and faced the threat. His intent was to return fire while attempting to move toward the alley for cover. He never made it. He knew something was wrong. All the time spent practicing his shooting skills in his basement. Still no chance. He automatically raised his left arm towards his head and face for protection.

Hot lead tore through the flesh of his forearms. Bam! Something slammed into his forehead. *Why can't I see out of my left eye? Holy shit! It feels like my eye is on fire and I can't move my left arm!*

Delloye realized that he had been shot more than once. Doing nothing at this point would have resulted in death, but his inherent fight or flight instincts took over and he acted. Delloye ran to the alley, only a few feet away, and found cover around the southwest corner of the bank.

Tommy gun fire would be sent his way but no other bullets found their mark. The piercing cries of ricochet rounds kept the adrenaline high alive and helped reduce the pain but not eliminate it. And it wouldn't stop the red flood pouring out of his head and eye. Delloye lowered himself to the concrete with his hands and knees finding a sense of safety and security on a stable surface. He lay in his now accumulating puddle of blood.

Helpless. Thinking about those people most important to him. "My wife, I can't give up now, my kids…" and his vision began fading to a calming white…

Although he didn't immediately realize it, sharp pieces of shattered glass ripped into DeNamur's right cheek. This was a mere flesh wound that wouldn't be fatal. DeNamur squared off to the Tommy gun while moving backward, returning fire with his feeble .38 Special. His heart rate increased to over 170 beats per minute, he began to suffer from common physiological anomalies that happen under combat stress.

"Why the hell am I going so slow?" he wondered. He sprinted backwards 100 feet past Schefe's Meat Market and to the U-shaped entrance of Tickler's Hardware.

It seemed to take forever.

Now behind cover he reloaded six rounds into the cylinder of his .38. Tommy rounds ricocheted off the concrete corner and near his feet.

"Why didn't I hear my gun go off…is this thing broke?" he thought to himself, suffering from auditory exclusion and unable to hear it. It's funny what happens under extreme stress. The body shuts down those senses that are not critical for survival and hearing is not needed to fight back.

"Damn it! The cops, the cops. Let's go, let's go!" the gangsters yelled as all three exited the bank to join the fire fight. They unloaded their Tommy guns south toward DeNamur and east across the street. DeNamur peeked around the corner, saw Tommy rounds passing just over his head and alongside him. He still managed to acquire his target and squeezed off six more from his .38.

"How the hell am I able to see those bullets whizzing past me?" he thought. Another change as survival mode kicked in. His visual clarity was enhanced. DeNamur then watched one of his bullets pierce a gangsters right shoulder.

The .38 slug entered the shoulder leaving a small hole, but flattened as it traveled through the body. It exploded out the back, spattering his blood in the air, marking the bank wall and sidewalk.

The gangster, realizing he was hit and screamed, "AR-GHHH! Damn it, I'm hit!" He was out of the battle and ran north on Broadway toward W. Mason Street. The trail of blood was easy to follow.

A piece of flying glass embedded in Hawley's chest as he exited the squad car. Oblivious to the pain, Hawley ran east across Broadway and stood behind a large tree. "I'm too old for this shit!" he thought to himself as he peeked out from behind the tree and squeezed off a couple of rounds from his shotgun. "This is not supposed to happen in my city…those bastards." He chambered another shell and fired it.

The gangsters took note of Hawley's position and delivered several indiscriminate Tommy rounds in his direction. Hawley could hear the rounds burrowing into the tree and he could not help but think about his "boys" under his command. "Are Burke, Delloye and DeNamur okay? Why are these bastards only shooting at me?" he thought as round after round continued cutting into the bark. The squad obstructed his view and he was unable to see Delloye lying in the alley. He looked over his left shoulder and could see DeNamur returning fire from the hardware store. He couldn't see Burke who was still inside the vehicle. "I pray that car has not become his coffin…" thought Hawley.

Hawley heard an obvious shriek of pain and looked to his right. Another ricochet round had found its mark. An innocent bystander, a man in his thirties gripped his chest, winced in pain and staggered away. A minor wound. No medical attention was needed and his name was never known.

Submachine gunfire was then directed away from Hawley and to his left, down the middle of Broadway. Riding his motorcycle with a sidecar, Raymond Arndt was mistaken for a police officer. Arndt drove right into the gunfight and several rounds skipped off the pavement and whizzed past his head. It was a sound a man never forgets. Arndt slammed on the brakes, screeched to a halt, abandoned his motorcycle, and ran east for cover, which he found inside a garage. The gangsters tracked Arndt while he ran and gunfire was directed right back at Hawley who thought to himself, "What kind of monsters have such reckless disregard for human life…to be shooting in the streets like this?"

Motorcycle officer Clem Faikel had answered the general alarm and approached from Broadway and Ninth Street, about a half mile south of the shootout. Upon Faikel's arrival, he saw the fire fight, drove his motorcycle off the road onto the sidewalk and laid it down near a tree that he used for cover.

"Chief, chief are you okay?" he asked Hawley, who was a tree or two to the north.

"I'm fine, I'm fine, just shoot those bastards!" Hawley demanded as the gangsters Nash began to drive away.

"Ha Ha Ha, it's hilarious when Dr. Clifford throws those fireworks from his office above the bank" 12-year-old Phillip Buck thought to himself, hearing the pops about a half block down the street from his father's grocery store. Dr. Clifford enjoyed dropping firecrackers out of his second floor window and frightening the sidewalk dwellers. The sounds continued in rapid succession and the boy stepped outside and saw the shootout. People along the streets scattered for their lives to find cover inside any available building or behind a tree. Some even jumped into cramped steel garbage cans, uncomfortable, but safe. Phillip watched it all unfold. Terrified screams could be heard in between the brief pauses of gunfire.

During Hawley and DeNamur's return fire, the wounded bandit ran right towards Phillip, but on the opposite side of the street. The boy stood in awe, *Holy cow, there's a robber and he's getting away,* he thought to himself. *If only I had a gun, I could pop him.*

He would never forget the gangster's appearance. He was an unmasked male with a darker complexion and Italian looking. He was short, about 5 feet tall with a medium build, wearing dark clothes. The most ominous image was this gangster carrying a Tommy gun by its handle with a 50-round drum attached.

The running gangster favored his right shoulder and appeared wounded. Blood was dripping from the arm. Buck watched him run west on W. Mason Street and then turned his attention back to the south. He would soon find himself inside a crime scene.

Driving east along W. Mason Street, Lloyd Delaruelle had the opportunity to bring the wounded gangster to justice or even to his grave. Delaruelle saw the gangster running right toward him on the sidewalk. *Take him out! Take him out!* Delaruelle thought to himself. A slight turn to the right would have steered his 2000-pound machine right into him. Preparing to do the unthinkable, Delaruelle glanced into his review mirror and saw a large black sedan rounding the corner at Chestnut Street. Presuming it was car load of more armed gangsters, he reconsidered, rapidly accelerated through a red light and continued over the river to the east side.

At the corner of Third Street and South Broadway stood the restaurant owner, J.B. McDermott. He had been inside and heard what sounded like a Fourth of July spectacle.

McDermott stepped outside and suddenly realized he was within 100 feet of the shootout. Completely unaware of the Tommy rounds coming his way, he watched Officer

DeNamur returning fire.

McDermott ran back to his restaurant to retrieve his gun. By the time he returned, the shooting was over and the Nash was leisurely pulling away. In shock from what he just witnessed, he stood frozen and didn't take any shots at the fleeing vehicle.

Detective Burke had nowhere to go and simply laid across the back seat in a fetal position with his hands over his head.

He prayed for the end.

Bullet after bullet passed over and through, slicing the quarter panels and shattering windows. He could only think about all those things he promised to do and would do if he somehow survived this. Once the bullets stopped flying overhead and he heard the gangsters' Nash accelerate south on Broadway, Burke emerged from the squad. He emptied his .38 caliber revolver into the Nash. A train blocked a southern escape route forcing the Nash to turn west on Third Street and out of sight.

Miraculously, the squad didn't become Burke's coffin. Outside of some minor cuts to his face caused by flying glass, he was unharmed!

"Jesus, thank God I'm alive!" Hawley muttered under his breath and removed his dark brown brimmed hat to rub his brow. "They must have been wearing armor" he wondered to himself a brief moment while surveying the scene. The bank was riddled with bullets, as was the squad car and businesses on both sides of the street.

"What the hell!" he exclaimed feeling and observing the hole in his hat just above the skull line. "That bullet just missed me…somebody was watching over me…" he thought until the screams of Detective Burke snapped him out of it.

Burke had just seen Delloye's lifeless body lying in the alley. Hawley had yet to realize there was a shard of glass embedded in his chest as well. Adrenaline is a great natural painkiller and that adrenaline high would sustain him while he ran to Delloye's aid.

Burke had turned to his right to scan for more gangsters and saw Delloye's silhouette in a puddle of blood. "Chief! Chief! August is down!" Burke yelled as he ran to and knelt alongside Delloye. Hawley and DeNamur would join him and nearing him in consternation, paused and stared for a brief moment at Delloye's large puddle of blood.

Delloye's pulse continued to pound, the arteries continued to move blood and life was quickly oozing out of him. Not much time.

Standing only a few feet away, young Phillip Buck stared at Delloye's bloodied body. In awe, he froze, stood there and watched, never believing that Delloye would live.

Not again.

They recalled Delloye's previous shooting only a few years prior. They all agreed that this didn't look good. They lifted a moaning Delloye into the back seat of a citizen's coach. Blood continued to pour from his left eye and shoulder. The surprised driver was ordered to take Delloye and DeNamur to the hospital and he willingly complied.

Frustrated and in rage, Hawley and Burke looked on with their blood-covered hands and watched Delloye driven away accompanied by DeNamur. They vowed to find the gangsters and bring them to justice. Hawley wondered how they would make the death notification to Delloye's wife and kids. All cops hope they never have to deliver that news.

A Death Notification...

"Mama, mama, do my hair?" called out tiny Laverne. She was the youngest child of seven, six sisters and one brother.

"Just a minute honey, mama's cooking. Papa is stopping home for lunch," said Clara Delloye. Tall, thin with sandy blonde hair styled in the 1930's coiffure — she was the wife of an officer — a role she proudly served. A beautiful young mother who kept her self busy with three young daughters and a strapping boy.

Laverne was a papa's girl, a spitting image of her mother. A wide smile that rounded off her glowing cheeks, the kind you wanted to pinch and say, "You're so cute." Papa adored her beautiful river blue-green eyes and blonde locks.

Papa, heroic on the job, and family man at home, liked to flip five-year-old Laverne's curls and braids with a finger. When she slept at night and before he went to bed, he pressed his large cop nose into those fresh-washed curls and relished the perfume scent.

"Smells good, Mama," said Laverne as she rounded the corner of the hallway into the kitchen of the Delloye home at 1168 E. Walnut Street on the city's east side. "You make my hair pretty for Papa?" the girl asked again.

She plopped herself up on a kitchen chair and waited patiently while her mother finished lunch preparation. "When's he coming home?" pouted Laverne. "At least two more hours Laverne, go on now. Busy yourself!" quipped her mother. She pulled out the sirloin roast she tended in the oven over the next hour.

It was now past 11:00 a.m. on that Monday morning, a hint of sun in the sky, the promise of a full sunny day. Harold, Delloye's fifteen-year-old son, was outside with friends riding his bike. He also liked to play an occasional game of horseshoes or take care of his carrier pigeons.

Adjusting his uniform and taking a deep breath, a uniformed officer slowly walked toward the front door of Delloye's modest home. A rectangular, grayish-blue wood-sided structure with peaks on both ends was well cared for. The matching wooden porch led up to the solid front door.

Taking the steps slowly, one at a time, the officer could be seen from inside through the picture window to his left. Prepared to deliver the news, the officer began to knock.

The smell of the pot roast filled the house. Knock, knock.

No answer. "Mama!" exclaimed Laverne walking to the living room.

"Not now Laverne!" said her mother, the hair standing up on the back of her neck. She felt that something was wrong, but ignored her intuition.

"Mama, somebody is at the door." Clara Delloye didn't immediately go to the door. Maybe it was a cops' wife instinct that stalled her.

Knock, knock.

Laverne peeked around the curtains of the front room and saw the uniform of a police officer.

"Mama!" she exclaimed again as Mrs. Delloye made her way to the door. She was wearing a light blue dress that day.

Laverne, not a shy child, put her small hand on her mother's skirt and together they both approached the door. Laverne gathered some of the blue material between her fingers *That's not my Papa,* she thought, not knowing her life was about to change forever.

Her hand began to quiver and she didn't know why…

En route to the hospital

DeNamur remained with Delloye and did his best, despite wet eyes, to reassure him that he was going to pull through. Delloye lay on his back and his head rested on DeNamur's lap. Blood engulfed Delloye's left eye, ran down his face, into his hair, soaked DeNamur's pant leg, and pooled on the back seat. His right eye stared straight back at DeNamur's face. Delloye continually slipped in and out of consciousness.

DeNamur's voice quivered, "Gus, you can't quit on us now. This is minor compared to the 177 rounds of buckshot you took in Preble…don't you give up, you understand, your wife and kids are counting on you…" he demanded upon arrival at St. Mary's Hospital on the city's east side. DeNamur, doctors, and nurses scooped up Delloye, placed him on a stretcher, and wheeled him into the operating room.

The bad news

Laverne continued to fidget while the wide-eyed officer took another deep breath and wet his lips to help him deliver a message that he had not prepared for that day. "May we speak alone?" the officer asked noticing Laverne at her mother's side. "Certainly," Clara Delloye choked out waving Laverne from her side.

The officer stepped in.

"I regret to inform you..." whispered the officer, his eyes darting to the right to catch a glimpse of Laverne still in the front room. Papa was a family man and all the force knew it. Nobody "wanted" to deliver this message, but somebody had to.

"I regret to inform you," he started again, "Gus has been injured and I must get you to the hospital."

Laverne's eyes were fixed on the back of Mama's blue dress a few feet away. The tall pretty frame of her mother began to heave forward and lose balance. The officer reached out to offer a steadying arm. Almost as quickly as she slumped, she straightened out again.

A brief pause and her mother turned slowly. She had to regain her composure for her children's sake and, after all, she was the wife of Detective Gus Delloye...

Back outside the South Side State Bank

Hawley took a deep breath to help gather his thoughts and contemplate his next move. He now had a major crime scene to deal with. His heart rate and breathing slowed and he came down from his adrenaline high returning blood to the surface of his skin. "My chest is killing me!" Hawley commented rubbing his left hand over it and now realizing he was bleeding.

He found a hole and presumed he was shot. A shard of

glass had driven deeply into his flesh. "Chief, they got you, too!" exclaimed Burke frantically commandeering another coach and convincing Hawley to get in.

"Damn it, Chief, get in...I will take over for now, you've got to get to the hospital!" Reluctant to leave the scene and his boys, he trusted Burke to get the job done and rode away to St. Vincent Hospital.

"Clink, Clang, Clink." The metal of the Tommy gun hit the concrete and the gangster knelt down to pick it up and thought, "Son of a bitch, I should just leave this money behind!" The gangster had a difficult time carrying the bag of money and the Tommy gun, but somehow managed. His obsession with money helped him get over the agonizing pain, which wasn't part of the plan. Nearly out of breath and still bleeding, the wounded gangster had run west on West Mason Street for a block and a half and then turned south down the alley between South Chestnut and South Maple Avenue. He ran to the alley between West Mason and Third Street; where Delloye, lying in his own blood, was now only a block and a half directly behind him.

Mrs. Henry Huth of 509 Third Street looked out her kitchen window and saw the gangster run right underneath it west through the alley. She immediately called the police department. His route didn't make much sense. He constantly scanned in all directions, appearing panicked and lost.

"Those bastards better not leave me behind," he thought as he ran to South Ashland Avenue and stopped for a brief moment. He could hear the footsteps and hollering of the armed posse seeking him. He would be shot and killed if they caught him.

"Where the hell are they?" he wondered, heading left and then right contemplating which way to run. Just then the Nash pulled up, he climbed inside and they sped off.

"You're bleeding quite a bit, pal," commented a fellow gangster. They helped the wounded gangster remove his blood-soaked suit coat.

"Damn, does this hurt!" He winced in pain and slowly moved his right arm out of the sleeve.

"Well, you got two holes in ya, one in the front and one coming out the back" observed one gangster looking at the entrance and exit wounds. "Better get some pressure on those holes to stop the bleeding." They pressed the now empty burlap money bag on his shoulder. Not a very porous compress, but it would do for now.

"This better be worth it," he said and sucked down some moonshine to dull the edge. "Hang in there, we got a long ride home…" commented the driver "…and the cops are not far behind!" Every agonizing bump in the road was felt and the wounded gangster drank the pain away.

Inside the Emergency Room

One look at Delloye's wounds made the diagnosis readily apparent to Dr. George Senn, "He's in critical condition," the doctor quietly mentioned to the nurse to avoid being overheard.

She recorded Delloye's present condition on the handwritten injuries report. "Patient brought to hospital after being shot in arm and head by robbers," she wrote until her concentration was broken by another voice.

"Doc, you better save him!" demanded DeNamur. Senn assured the officer he would do his best. DeNamur walked out of the operating room mumbling some words to God. He headed back to the scene.

"We need X-ray's now to see where the bullets are," demanded Dr. Senn. They put direct pressure on Delloye's left eye and shoulder and wrapped up his left forearm. He was wheeled to X-ray with doctors and nurses walking alongside, maintaining pressure, and doing their best to stop the bleeding.

A few minutes later the internal photographs revealed

damning injuries. "Several small pellets, buckshot or small pellets size of .22 — One large bullet over left orbital socket." These .22-caliber pellets were left over from his previous shooting a few years ago, but the one behind his eye was a gangster's .45-caliber slug. Although conscious, Delloye's respirations and heart rate were slow. His thoughts would continue to focus on his family.

Mama has to go now...

"Laverne, something has happened at the police department and I must leave for a time," said Clara Delloye, as young Laverne moved back toward her.

"What's wrong, Mama?" she quivered.

"I'm not sure yet, honey, but I need you not to worry. Everything will be okay. Your sister Margaret will take care of you, I will be home in a little while."

Clara Delloye was trying to control the lump building in her throat. The tiniest of pools began to gather in the wells of her eyes. Tears rolled down her cheeks while she readied herself to leave. *Compose yourself,* she thought, *You're the wife of a detective.*

Mrs. Delloye had spent a decade preparing for this and she had been there before three years ago. *Keep it together, no emotions, you can do it, hang on,* she reminded herself.

"Mama, I'm scared. Is Papa coming home?" asked Laverne, "What's happening?"

Mrs. Delloye hugged her daughter firmly and then pulled away. Time was precious. She knew her husband's life was in the balance.

Mrs. Delloye looked back one last time as her hand grabbed for the door. Grief. Fear. Whatever it was, she couldn't even see the handle but could feel it.

Laverne sobbed and her mother could see her lips trembling, but the cries were muttered. When the door opened, Laverne stood with her tearful eyes fixed on it, until it slowly shut.

Mrs. Delloye was ushered into an awaiting squad car. The race was on. "Get me there! I need to be with him!" demanded Mrs. Delloye. "Yes ma'am…" replied the officer and they raced toward St. Mary's Hospital.

"These dressings are saturated," the nurse mumbled to herself as she removed the now-yellowed cloth from Delloye's left eye and replaced it with a clean white one. This would continue throughout the night as yellow fluid from his injured eyeball continually seeped. Morphine and cold compresses were added to help reduce the pain and discomfort, but Delloye would have a difficult time resting…

The Crime Scene

Detective Burke and Officer Faikel now had a major crime scene on their hands. Hundreds of curious onlookers filled the streets, walking in and around the bank, contaminating the scene. Some stepped in blood, while others inadvertently kicked empty shell casings. Many more stood in awe viewing the bullet-riddled police car. This was a regular event in Chicago, but not in this small town. Scene control, communications, and manpower were lacking.

Burke hurried inside the bank and called the police department. "Patton, Gus is shot, pretty bad, and Hawley's in the hospital too…not as bad though. Get me all officers here now! And tell WHBY radio about it! Get this broadcasted to all agencies west of us! They were Italian-looking gangsters, younger, maybe in their 30's, wearing suits, one had a straw hat and he was shot — bleeding badly. They were driving dark colored cars, Arrows or Nashes. I will get you more later!" and he slammed down the phone.

Burke's turned his attention towards Sager and Geraldine Miller. Both were still sobbing. He walked over to them and also saw Cayer on the floor. He was slowly coming to in his puddle of blood. "Please check the vault…they beat Mr. Slupinski in there, I think he's dead," cried Sager.

The vault door was wide open. Burke rushed in and found Slupinski suffering the aftermath of a severe beating.

Slupinski was crumpled on the floor in his dark suit and carefully placed tie, recalled his 102-year-old widow Julia. "He didn't know what had happened. He was in a daze. My, didn't those fellows have the nerve robbing like that before noon." She shook her head. "I didn't expect a robbery that day. I was all involved with the baby. What a day! He came home and told me there was a robbery. That is how I found out."

At the bank, Slupinski pulled himself up and Burke escorted him outside.

Sgt. Patton had sounded the citywide alarm. All call boxes in the city rang and notified officers to respond. Fifteen uniform officers, about half the force, began to arrive, some on foot and others in their personal cars. The wool police blue uniform and silver tin badges stood out. They immediately began to help.

A few entered the bank and began herding the bystanders out the door. Another drove Slupinski to the hospital. Cayer was helped to his feet and also driven away. In a feeble attempt to preserve evidence, officers outside did their best to keep the curious away from the shot-up squad car and scattered shell casings. No doubt a few shell casings became souvenirs. There were just too many people around.

Completely securing the crime scene was impossible. All members of the police department, including those on leave, eventually arrived and helped as best they could. Local fingerprint expert Detective Otto Cronce checked for latent prints. He dusted the obvious areas, the door, the counter tops, and the vault shelves, covering them with thin layers of black powder. With the number of people that had been inside the bank since the robbery, if any prints were found, it would be a daunting task to determine if they belonged to civilians or suspects.

Burke grabbed some paperwork from the squad car and

walked back into the bank. He knelt down beside Sager, who was beginning to compose herself. Tears slowly ran down her cheeks. Geraldine Miller was gone and Burke presumed she ran home. "You're going to be okay, they're gone, I'm a detective" Burke said, doing his best to reassure and comfort the woman. "Let me help you to your feet," he suggested while assisting with his hands underneath her right arm and shoulder.

Unsteady, Sager slowly stood up. Burke walked her to the cashier's desk and she carefully sat down in a creaky wooden chair. Burke asked her what happened and quickly recorded the following written statement:

It is July 20, 1931, at 11:30 a.m. and this is a statement from Bernice Sager:

It was about a half-hour ago. We were all inside the bank when all of a sudden I saw two men jumping over the railing and ordering us out of the cages. I didn't get a real good look at their faces. They were well-dressed, white men, in their 20s and 30s, and wore nice double-breasted suits. They took me and threw me on the floor, along with the others. Another one stayed at the door. I think he was the leader. He gave most of the commands. They all had guns, big ones with a round cylinder underneath them. They forced Frank Slupinski into the vault and then beat him. I could hear him moaning. They also beat Earl Cayer over the head while he was right next to me. Earl's head was bleeding all over and he wasn't moving. Then they began to panic, like something was wrong. They filled a sack with money and ran outside. I heard lots of loud pops and assumed it was gunfire. I prayed that the police were here. Lucky I was a girl or I would have got a beating, too. I have never been more terrified in my life.

Signed: Bernice Sager
Written By: Captain Burke

(**AUTHOR'S NOTE:** The above is is a recreated written statement, based upon factual information provided by Bernice Sager, which was likely taken by Captain Burke.)

Burke walked Sager outside. "We will call you when we get these guys" he said.

She walked away and into the crowd towards her apartment to the north. Burke knelt down and picked up a few shell casings.

There were hundreds from which to choose. At the same time he looked, in disbelief, at the squad car, full of holes a few feet to his right. *How the hell did we survive this,* he wondered.

He squinted into the sunlight across the street to see shattered windows and bullet holes in business after business. His trance lasted only a few seconds. Feeling a touch on his left shoulder and the frantic voice of a middle-aged woman snapped him out of it.

"Officer! Officer! I saw the whole thing," said Mrs. Malchow, the wife of an assemblyman, whose voice inflection varied somewhere between anxiety and giddiness. She wouldn't allow Burke to say a word while explaining, "I got stuck in my vehicle by Mason Street. I thought it was fireworks, but then I saw a man running from the bank. He...he was carrying a bag and ran into a car. A large black one from which another man was shooting. The car sped off...that way, that way (while pointing west towards Ashland Avenue). I also saw an officer shooting at them from behind a tree across the street..." Burke interrupted her.

"Ma'am, I appreciate it, but can you tell me what the bandits looked like?" he politely asked.

"No, I was too excited to notice anything like that," she explained.

Burke couldn't help it. *Unbelievable.* He smirked. He wrote down her name, thanked her for the help and sent her on her way.

Burke walked to the squad and cautiously sat in the driver's seat. He didn't want to disturb any potential evidence. At the same time, he needed to get it out of the street and to a more secluded area. He never heard the hundreds of voices still talking about what they just saw. He drove it around to the back of the bank and parked it in the alley. He assigned a uniform officer to guard it and he continued his scene investigation.

Burke returned to the front of the bank and began following the blood trail that led north on Broadway towards Mason Street. It wasn't much different than tracking a seriously wounded deer. The red droplets followed the bandits' path exactly.

Burke kept an eye out for more physical evidence and didn't find any. When he arrived at the sidewalk along South Ashland where the injured bandit was picked up, a small pool of blood was there. He concluded that the bandit remained somewhat stationary for a short period of time, allowing the blood to gather. He was miffed that the bandit had gotten away and subconsciously hoped he would get his just desserts — that being death.

(AUTHOR'S NOTE: Blood didn't hold the same evidentiary value that it does today. Blood typing existed, but it was not a valid or conclusive means of positively identifying somebody. DNA was unheard of at that time.)

The phone calls poured into the police department and Sgt. Patton had a difficult time keeping up. News reporters, nosy citizens, family members, and witnesses - they kept calling. He would hang up the phone, scribble down some notes, only for it to ring again. This continued for hours. He did his best to write down worthy information and recorded the following tips:

• 11:16 a.m. — Mrs. Henry Huth, 508 Third St., saw wounded bandit run down alley past her house. He was of medium build, wearing a reddish brown suit and straw hat. Looked like he was shot in the right arm. Blood soaked through his coat sleeve. Can't identify him, but can recognize his clothing. She also heard him drop something, sounded like metal — might have been a machine gun. He picked it up with his left hand and ran north on Maple. Haven't seen him since.

• 11:20 a.m. — Al DeGroot of DeGroot & Allen electric saw a dark Nash sedan, bearing an Illinois license plate — first two numbers of "48." It was speeding north on 12ᵗʰ (just west of Ashland) and almost hit him as he crossed the street. It blared its horn at him and he jumped back. One man was in the front seat driving and two others were bending over in the back seat, possibly working over another lying on the floor.

• 11:23 a.m. — Frank Garhusky, mechanic of Pankratz Motor Car Company, saw the bandits leave the bank after the robbery. They were driving a maroon 1929 Studebaker President sedan with a trunk on the back. Unknown license plate number.

• 11:25 a.m. — Mrs. George Vandenboom, 700 S. Maple Ave., saw two cars speeding down Maple Avenue and saw a wounded bandit picked up by a maroon car (Studebaker?)…Mr Lonquist, 701 S. Maple, also on the line…saw blood streaming down the right elbow of a wounded man as he got in the car. A dark blue Nash was following.

Burke had walked through the alley, past Delloye's pool of blood, and back to the front of the bank. A frantic E.J. Van Vondern, the head cashier, walked up to Burke. "Detective! Detective! Is everybody okay?" he asked anxiously. Burke paused to gather his thoughts and replied, "Couple of your employees are in the hospital…they should be okay…and… Gus, one of our guys, he was shot, might die. I need you to get in the bank and figure out how much is missing."

Von Vondern hurried into the bank, but when he passed through the heavy wooden doors, he suddenly slowed. The trails and puddles of blood on the wooden floor shocked the conscious and he imagined the wounds they came from.

Every step seemed so slow while he avoided the dime size droplets that came from the heads of Slupinski and Cayer. Von Vondern walked behind the cage and into the vault.

He stopped, gasped, and swallowed hard.

Blood, currency, securities, deposit slips, change — it was everywhere.

The pool of blood where Slupinski once lay was like a coagulated mass of gelatin. Blood splattered and sprayed the vault walls and shelving. His thoughts clouded, Von Vondern had difficulty remembering his simple task. That was to count the money and find out how much was missing.

All the securities and small amounts of gold were accounted for. A quick count of the cash on hand revealed about $10,000 missing. He passed this onto Burke, cleaned up the bank, and within a few hours it was business as usual.

Burke cautiously drove the squad car around the thrill seekers. They pointed in amazement as he proceeded north on Broadway and east on Mason Street towards the police department. The jailbirds below, alerted by the commotion above, watched from their perches while Burke drove by. At least they all had solid alibis and couldn't be pinched for this one. He parked the squad in the police garage, collected some Tommy gun bullets lying around the passenger compartment, walked past the city jail cells, went upstairs and inside.

Officer Patton updated him with the latest tips and new developments. "We have 32 members of the Brown County Vigilantes, armed with machine guns, out to the west looking and waiting for any new information. They will periodically call in. The Fire Chief, Ralph Drum, he volunteered to help and is up in a plane with a pilot and…"

Burke interrupted him, "The fire chief? What? Doesn't

he put out fires?"

Patton snickered, "Relax Burke, he is a trained artillery man from the world war, plus he has a machine gun."

Satisfied, Burke urged Patton to continue. "And, De-Namur left Gus at the hospital, stopped here for a bit, sent a car to get Gus' wife to the hospital, and he is also up in a plane, with a machine gun, searching for the gangsters. I have also notified all agencies in the area and they are all volunteering to help. WHBY is also broadcasting this…"

The phone rang and interrupted them. "Hello," the excited man's voice continued. "I live on the west side, off of Taylor Street. There is an auto parked in the woods with three men in it. I think two of them are wounded…" Burke inquired for more information, color of the car, descriptions of the men, but this was it. Within an hour, the posse called for an update and this tip was passed onto them.

Burke phoned Chief Hawley at the hospital and updated him as well. Hawley encouraged Burke to press on and make sure the bandits were apprehended. Hawley also reminded Burke to notify the Wisconsin Banker's Association right away. Their investigators wouldn't assist if they were not notified within 10 days. Burke set the phone down and it immediately rang again. "Detective Burke please," head cashier Von Vondern requested. "Speaking," replied Burke. "We made a mistake, there's actually $6,995 missing. We are sure of it." Burke recorded the revised figure and thanked Von Vondern for the update.

Now 1 p.m., Gus Delloye remained in serious condition. "Get the Mayo Clinic on the line, we need an expert here!" Dr. Senn knew Delloye's eye injury was serious and it would probably have to be removed. Extreme pain, burning pain, pressure pain — it would last throughout the night.

Continuous doses of morphine would help a bit and only exhaustion allowed him to sleep for short periods. The bleeding continued for nine hours and finally stopped.

Mrs. Delloye remained by her husband's side until late and was then driven home to tell the kids, as best she could, that their papa would pull through. St. Mary's Hospital, room 103, would be Delloye's new home address for the next month.

The posse arrived in the wooded area off of Taylor Street. They hoped this tip would be their last. 3:00pm would be a perfect time to hang it up for the day. They rolled to a stop at the car-sized path that led into the woods. The dark colored vehicle they hoped to see was still there, facing them, about twenty-five feet into the trees. A dark colored Nash or Chevrolet coach, it didn't matter, just so it contained the wanted men.

"There they are! There they are!" The posse saw them. The sunlight glared into their eyes and they couldn't see if the gangsters were inside it. Posse members began to exit their cars and cautiously approach. Occupied by three people, the car's engine started up, rapidly accelerated and the car sped past them. The spinning tires spit dust, dirt, and rocks into the air. Surprised, the posse members didn't expect such a quick escape and scrambled to get back in their cars and pursue.

The chase was on. The gangsters wouldn't be allowed to escape if posse members had anything to do with it. The bumpy dirt roads made it easy for the posse to follow the gangster's machine — they just followed the dust. Closer and closer, the posse caught up. The gangsters slid to a stop. The posse slid to a stop. They outnumbered the gangsters and planned to end it quickly.

"Get your hands up! Get your hands up! Get out of the car! Get out of the car!" Posse members barked out orders and fearing for their lives, the occupants complied. Slowly, first the driver, then the front passenger stumbled out. Their hands reached for the sky.

"Don't hurt me! Don't hurt me!" The voice of a female screeched from the back seat.

"You, too, get out!" demanded a posse member. Frozen in

fear, the woman had difficulty complying or, for that matter, even thinking.

"A keg of beer" one posse member quipped, spotting the keg in the back seat.

"You mean you're not the drys?" the driver nervously asked referring to the prohibition hit squad affectionately known as "dry agents."

Frustrated, another replied, "We're looking for some bank robbers and you're obviously not them."

The posse patted down the three suspects, who weren't injured, and then searched the car. Nothing was found except for the beer, which the posse left behind.

"We're sorry to cause such trouble," said the driver.

"Next time, don't run and you'll save us all a lot of trouble," a posse member said. "Get the hell out of here." The posse went one way and the federal law violators another.

Another tip came in by phone. Sgt. Patton noted it and ordered three uniform officers to track it down. "We just had a bus driver call us. A little while ago he saw a car, a black one, west on Hwy. 29, west of the city near Burdon's Hill," he said. "The windshield was shattered and it was speeding."

The officers sped out of the parking lot, through downtown streets west on Hwy. 29. Patton also notified the Shawano County Sheriff's Department. They were all too late. A patrol officer phoned and expressed his frustrations, "Damn it Patton! This would be a lot easier if we had the radio equipment that the chief has been requesting. This better be a wake-up call! The common council oughta approve these funds now!" The phone went dead. The gangsters had eluded them again.

Law enforcement from jurisdictions all around northeast Wisconsin monitored main roads and major intersections. The bandits' escape was well planned and they likely took desolate country roads back to their safe house.

Dusk settled in and night soon followed. The gangsters

were still on the loose.

Just when the police were about to give up for the night, a promising lead was phoned in. An anonymous caller from Denmark, a rural community about ten miles south of the city, reported that two vehicles had dropped off a wounded man inside a barn at a certain farmyard.

Brown County deputies quickly responded. Their two squads skidded to a stop outside the closed wooden barn doors. With guns in hand, deputies cautiously approached and slowly pulled opened the doors.

Distinct snoring could be heard from inside. Any pleasant dream about spending his loot soon turned into a nightmare when the deputies ordered him to awake.

Startled, the lethargic grown man slowly stood up and fell over again. He wasn't injured, but had consumed a little too much of the "devils urine" and was obviously drunk. He wasn't a bank robber. Frustrated, the deputies pushed him into a squad and dropped him off at the city jail.

Sheriff's deputies and vigilantes came in empty handed at about 11:30 p.m. City officers covered over 300 miles of roads and returned after midnight. No sight of the gangsters.

Burke worked late that night and with Hawley's input they began to theorize who may have done this. Gangsters from Illinois? A logical conclusion, after all, the most well known bank robber, Dillinger, had a reason to come to Green Bay. He would visit one of his many girlfriends. Plus one of the witnesses reported a Nash with Illinois plates. Their efforts would be temporarily, but inaccurately, focused towards the south.

The wounded gangster, still inside the fleeing machine, was not doing so well. Barely awake, mumbling his words, slipping into unconsciousness. The bright red blood lost from his shoulder was great. It was likely an arterial wound that just wouldn't stop "He doesn't look good, boys," commented one. Gangster and ethics didn't go hand in hand.

"No man left behind" was an optional credo. They sped over the Mississippi River, into Minnesota, and came to a stop. The wounded gangster was rolled out of the passenger side of the car and into a ditch.

Written accounts and interviews indicate that a man with wounds matching those of the injured gangster was found dead near the Wisconsin and Minnesota border several days after the robbery. Coroner records in both states have been unable to confirm this.

Tuesday, July 21, 1931

"Two Arrested in S.S. Bank Holdup" — Green Bay Press Gazette

"How the hell are we going to get back to St. Paul," John Libgott and Bill Carney wondered as they walked the streets of Appleton, Wisconsin — a half-hour south of Green Bay. Both of them, barely 18 years old, had bummed their way to this tiny town. They had left their hotel a few hours ago, found a safe house, drank a bit, and were now aimlessly wandering Appleton's quiet and empty downtown streets.

Standing beneath a streetlight, mid-block along College Avenue, they caught the beat cop's eye. "Gentlemen, it's 4 a.m., what ya up to?" inquired the constable on patrol. Libgott and Carney had difficulty getting their stories straight and provided conflicting information. One said they had hitchhiked from St. Paul and the other said they had beat their way on a freight. They both also happened to be of dark complexion, "Italian-looking," and seemed a bit nervous. Aware of the Green Bay bank robbery, they were detained and escorted to the Appleton Police Department.

A couple hours later Appleton Police Chief Prim phoned the Green Bay Police. Burke requested Libgott and Carney's presence. Hoping he had the right guys, Chief Prim was happy to oblige.

In the meantime, Burke had plenty of other things to do. Sift through all the leads, keep his troops, other agencies and the vigilantes up-to-date, address the media — print and radio - and explain the incident again and again to every curious citizen who walked in. Frankly, Burke was tired of repeating himself. He opened the police garage and let the citizens file through to view the shot-up squad car and satisfy their appetite.

It didn't take long for the word to get out. Soon, lines snaked out of the police garage and into the parking lot. Everybody wanted a front-row view. Those that saw it had a story to tell, some more exaggerated than others.

Burke drove to St. Mary's to visit Delloye and waited outside his room while he was being cared for. The rays of the rising sun were suppressed by drawn shades to prevent Delloye's eyes from their involuntary squint. Dr. Senn carefully examined Delloye's eye and confirmed his fears — he was unable to save it. He did the best he could to stabilize Delloye until the specialist arrived. The detective's pulse had improved, but he remained restless throughout the day, sleeping in short intervals and waking for sips of water or an ice bag on his head before falling back asleep. Morphine remained his best friend. Delloye would never recall these first two days in the hospital. The visits by family, friends, and co-workers…

Burke only stayed a few minutes. He couldn't bear it. Delloye's swollen, bruised and bloodied face altered his appearance and made him somewhat unrecognizable. Burke walked out praying that Delloye would make it.

Burke then visited Hawley, whose condition was much improved. Hawley joked about still being in the hospital for such a mere flesh wound and didn't want anybody to worry about him. It was too late for that. Word had gotten back to everybody at the police department about the near rollover crash almost caused by Hawley's son when the news of his injury became known.

"Your son, the one on James Street, after he heard your were injured, came driving around the corner near his house, skidding sideways, and blew out a tire," Burke said. "Your grandkids were playing in the front yard and saw it all. They're on their way here to see you."

Hawley chuckled at the news. "At least it will give them something to talk about." They chatted about the robbery for a little while, made sure they were on the same page, and then parted.

Burke arrived at the police department and again briefed all of the officers, many of who were volunteering their time to help out. WHBY radio and the *Green Bay Press-Gazette* continued spreading the word. The vigilantes were out again searching wooded areas to the west.

Sticks snapping, underbrush and leaves rustling, insects buzzing, July heat in Wisconsin brings the woods to life. This made searching for the bandits a daunting challenge, but the prize was worth the effort.

What vigilante in their right mind wouldn't want the bragging rights for capturing a gangster?

They conducted field searches in an organized fashion. Vigilantes formed a line, a few feet apart from each other, and walked in unison. This ensured that large areas were thoroughly, yet efficiently searched. Like hunting deer or flushing out pheasants, much time could be spent with little to no results.

Hunting man was a bit different.

They can shoot back.

"Hey! Hey! Look to your right," whispered one vigilante to another. "There! There, on his belly, in the brush."

A dark suit coat and white undershirt could be seen. The wounded, possibly deceased gangster had finally been found. Three vigilantes approached with caution. They firmly gripped their weapons and raised them towards the target.

The pads of their right index fingers were poised to crush the triggers and, if necessary, destroy their foe. Their breathing became deeper, heart rates increased, and tunnel vision set in.

They were focused and ready for the test. Ten feet, nine feet, eight feet...they continued closing the gap. "Moo! Moooo!" the frightened cow quickly rolled to its feet and ran away. Startled, the vigilantes jumped back, nearly falling, but maintaining their balance. Thankfully, neither of them accidentally discharged their weapons. "That was utterly amazing," one said sarcastically while others moaned at his play on words. This story would be retold time and again. The wounded gangster wouldn't be found.

"Green Bay Police, Det. Burke," he answered the phone. He recorded another tip that seemed to explain how the gangsters disappeared so quickly. The excited caller reported, "This is Mr. Lehey from the farm on Taylor and Mason. I just heard the radio broadcast of the robbery and while getting the mail yesterday, saw something that you might be interested in."

Burke perked up, leaned forward in his chair, and listened intently. Lehey continued: "It was about 11:30 a.m. I saw a semi-truck with a covered ramp or trailer attached to it. A dark-colored machine drove into it. Within a few seconds, a couple of cops on motorcycles flew right past it. I didn't think much of it until I heard the radio broadcast today. I'm sorry I didn't call sooner. I hope this helps."

Burke pried for more information, a more thorough vehicle description, a more complete description of the driver or passengers. He needed more. Nothing available. Burke thanked the man for calling and hung up.

At about 2 p.m., Chief Prim arrived. He had personally driven Libgott and Carney and happily turned them over to Burke. They were led to a holding cell and asked the reason why. Somewhat terse and direct, Burke replied, "Robbing a bank, shooting some cops, you know anything about that?" Clueless, both of them denied involvement but Burke wasn't buying it and closed the iron door behind them.

Burke, along with Green Bay's two other detectives, Frank Morgan and John Taylor, clarified the details of the apprehension with Chief Prim. Burke agreed, their conflicting stories were concerning. However, there was no indication, at this point, that they were involved in yesterday's terror.

Morgan and Taylor left the department and returned some 20 minutes later with Slupinski and Cayer. With their swollen, bruised, and battered faces, they both viewed Libgott and Carney.

"No, it's not them, they are too young, much younger then the robbers," stated Slupinski. Cayer agreed. Despite their inability to positively identify Libgott and Carney, Detectives Morgan and Taylor still interrogated them.

"Where were you yesterday?"

"Who can confirm that?"

"Why would the witnesses say you were at the bank when it was robbed?"

"Admit it, get it off your chest, you know you were involved."

"If you continue to bullshit me, I will personally see to it that you are put away a long time!" Morgan and Taylor fired at the two.

Good cop, bad cop, subterfuge, heavy-handed, empathetic, emotional appeals — they tried all the angles. Libgott and Carney consistently denied involvement. Convinced and lacking any real proof, Burke had no other choice but to release them.

Slupinski and Cayer were waiting in the police lobby. Disappointed, Burke told them that their suspects were not involved and would be released. They understood and opened the door to leave, holding it for another man who was walking in.

"Excuse me, are you Detective Burke?" he asked.

"You got 'im." Burke replied.

"Hello, sorry to hear about your guys that were shot, hope they will be okay. I'm A.M. DeVoursney, detective, Wisconsin Bankers Association."

The Federal Bureau of Investigation had yet to investigate bank robberies and was too busy chasing moonshiners and liquor runners. Investigators from the Wisconsin Bankers Association (WBA) and the American Bankers Association (ABA) were the experts in this field.

"Ah yes, we were expecting you, thank you for coming. Wait a second!" Burke hurried outside and hollered for Slupinski and Cayer to come back. Catching them just in time, they walked back in and were introduced to DeVoursney.

"Here, thumb through this book and tell me if anybody looks familiar to you." DeVoursney handed them a photo album of several known bank robbers. Hopefully they would be able to identify some or even one of them.

A few minutes passed. "We're sorry guys, but none of these bandits were the ones that we saw," said Cayer while he handed the album back to DeVoursney.

"Thanks again" Burke said softly and bid them good night as they left. This time it was for good.

Burke updated DeVoursney and recounted the robbery, leads, developments, and the arrests and release of Libgott and Carney. DeVoursney had never heard of Libgott and Carney and agreed with Burke, they were probably not involved.

They were interrupted when Brown County Undersheriff Coleman stopped in and provided yet another update. "I just got back in from Shawano. We were checking some cottages of some known Chicago gangsters, namely Joe Saltis' place. It was empty. Town folk haven't seen him for weeks." Burke thanked him for the update and he left.

De Voursney explained to Burke, "Saltis isn't your typical

bank robber, but rather a rum runner. He's connected with Capone. They don't rob banks. They just kill their competition. You know, like all good businessmen do. But Dillinger, now that is a possibility."

BRRRING...BRRRING! They were interrupted by yet another caller with a tip. An excited voice reported, "I just heard a loud bang, like gunshots on the southeast side of the city. You better send someone to check it out."

"Yes, sir" Burke replied, hanging up the phone. He turned to DeVoursney, "Now people are reporting more gunshots... one robbery and now firecrackers scare them..."

BRRRING...BRRRING! The phone ran again, then again, and continued to at least once a minute for the next hour. Caller after caller reported these same gunshots. After the third call, Burke, with no other choice, sent two officers to the southeast side of the Fox River to check it out. They reported back a few minutes later by phone, "Captain, it's just the Legion members practicing for their WWI performance. Now you and the people can relax."

The shots-fired call reminded Burke of some evidence he needed to pass on. He gave De Voursney a couple shell casings and bullets from the bank robbery scene. De Voursney immediately recognized them as a typical round fired from the underbelly of the Tommy gun. Burke also helped make arrangements for Ms. Sager to view the photo album.

She, too, was unable to positively identify any of the known robbers. Dead end after dead end, the investigation was becoming very frustrating. As more and more time passed by, the chances of apprehending the gangsters became less and less. De Voursney spent the night in Green Bay, visited the scene, and talked to bystanders — anybody who could provide information. He also coordinated his efforts with O.W. Ahearn, an investigator with the American Bankers Association. They both stayed a few days, assisted as much as they could, and left empty-handed.

City Council Session / 7 p.m.

Commotion filled the city council chambers. The bank robbery was the main topic of conversation. Mayor John V. Diener pounded the wooden gavel and called the session to order. The city treasurer's report was received and discussed, followed by a report "Regarding Providing Funds for Police Department." Five councilmen were of the opinion that the funds were no longer available for the continuance of the (four) extra policemen now employed or for installation of a much needed police radio system. Infuriated, Aldermen Clement Dwyer stood to his feet and delivered his finest monologue to date.

"At the present time our chief and captain are suffering from wounds and Lieutenant Delloye lies in a local hospital in critical condition, the sight of one eye gone forever. These injuries being received in a battle with a gang of bandits, the likes of which this city, county, and even our state, have never seen before. Chief Thomas Hawley has steadfastly stood by his department and without a word of complaint has maintained his department and protected the lives and property of the citizens of our city on a budget far too small for the people and territory to be protected. Although reports of the battle are mixed and confused, when sifted down and the actual facts are obtained, our Chief and the rest of his men battled these bandits in a manner that was a tribute to the department and a credit to themselves. Had they displayed the same valor in any of our wars they would undoubtedly been recognized for bravery. We cannot ask or expect either the chief or his men to again risk their lives as they did on the morning of July 20 It is our duty to them and to our citizens to man sufficient men for the proper protection of our city and properly equip those men with new and modern ways of crime detection and prevention. In the late war we did not send our boys to the front lines with slingshots or peashooters, but put into their hands for use the most modern and up-to-date equipments of war that could be secured. The Police Department of this city and every other city is constantly at war with crime detention, detection, and apprehension. Needless to say, those who duty it is to take care of this situation should be properly manned and equipped…"

Aldermen Dwyer concluded by explaining where the funds could be appropriated from and with a deep breath and watery eyes, he scanned the room looking at his fellow elected officials and sat down. His motion was seconded and carried. Modernizing the Green Bay Police was born. Unfortunately, it took a tragedy for the council to be educated and make an informed decision.

Wednesday, July 22, 1931

At 6 a.m., Delloye's eyelids fluttered and he could barely hear the voice speaking softly in his right ear. "Don't let them chisel those slugs out of your head," whispered Mayo Clinic specialist Dr. George Seering.

Analysis of the X-rays revealed a .45-caliber bullet lodged between Delloye's left orbital socket and skull. It didn't penetrate the skull but was near vital structures and would be too risky to remove. The wounds to his bandaged left arm would heal on their own; the bullets had passed right through it. But his eye was another matter. The Mayo Clinic surgeon agreed, the eye couldn't be saved. The bullet and shards of glass had caused too much damage. In order to avoid sympathetic inflammation of the remaining right eye, the damaged and now useless left eye would have to be removed ASAP.

Delloye opened his eyes, only seeing out of his right one. He squinted. The white walls made the light seem so bright. At the foot of his bed, on the wall near the ceiling, a bronze-colored cross was mounted.

Sitting at Delloye's bedside, Dr. Seering explained the

A 1921 Thompson "Tommy" submachine gun (No. 9055), which was donated to the Green Bay Police Department by a local bankers association. The Tommy gun was the weapon of choice for many Depression-era bank robbers and outlaws. (Photo by Mike R. Knetzger, enhanced by Jeremy A. Muraski.)

medical necessity of the procedure. The detective listened intently, remaining silent. "Gus, your left eye is badly damaged and you will never be able to see out of it again. A half-inch shard of glass penetrated it and lodged in your cornea, and fluid is leaking out of your eye. We need to remove the eye to prevent any sympathetic inflammation of your right eye. In other words, your right eye will have *sympathy* for your damaged one and also become inflamed. Your right eye could also possible suffer from redness, hypersensitivity to light, blurred vision, or even loss of vision. We want to avoid that. This is a relatively simple procedure that takes about an hour. You'll be under full anesthesia and won't feel any pain. Once the damaged eye is removed, I will eventually replace it with a cosmetic glass eye that will, to a great extent, match your right eye. The cosmetic eye will be inserted in about two to four weeks. In the meantime, a temporary plastic insert called a conformer will be inserted to maintain the shape of your eye and surrounding tissue. You'll be given medication for any pain and discomfort. X-rays show that the bullet entered just above your left eye and is lodged in the bones of your skull. As of now, we are not going to remove the bullet because it is too risky. The bullet will not rust and shouldn't cause any permanent damage or discomfort. I'll clean up the arm wounds and they should heal on their own. Now, what questions do you have for me?"

This was a lot for Delloye to take in but he understood why his damaged and now useless left eye needed to be removed. He couldn't see out of it and it was causing considerable pain and discomfort. Delloye was a bit baffled about the bullet remaining in his head. "So, the bullet is staying in my head…why is it too risky to remove?"

Dr. Seering replied, "The bullet is lodged between your skull and nasal bones, behind the orbital socket. To remove it would require considerable surgery, cutting through bones and nasal cavities in order to get at it. Furthermore, it's too close to optic fibers from your other eye and if we damage them you might be totally blind. Leaving it in won't pose any significant risk. You'll likely have headaches for a couple of weeks until the internal swelling and inflammation subsides."

"One more thing," the detective said. "Can I get something to eat? I'm starving." Unable to have solids before surgery, he consumed two servings of milk and some vanilla ice cream. Anything would do.

Dr. Seering concluded, "Okay Gus, I will see you again around 6 p.m, when we'll begin the procedure. Do the best you can to get some rest and let your nurse know if you have any additional questions." Dr. Seering then met with Mrs. Delloye and also explained the medical procedures to her.

Delloye frequently requested to see his wife and privately they both wondered if his life would ever be the same. Could he garden again like he did every morning after finishing the night shift? Gardening was not only his hobby, but also a significant source of food — potatoes, peas, carrots, onions, and tomatoes — that fed his family well. Would he play with his kids? See them grow up? Would his wife see him through another tragedy? Would he have to retire?

His wife squeezed Delloye's right hand and kissed him on the forehead. "I love you, Gus. We are going to make it through this. I will always be here for you." Two tears, one from each eye, slowly ran down her face. "I will be here all day and until I know you made it out of surgery okay. The kids are taken care of and they're praying for you. I'm praying for you. Everybody is praying for you." Comforted, her love and words sustained him. "I love you, too." he whispered. They spent the rest of the day together.

It was time. In the operating room, Delloye stared at the mask being fitted over his nose and mouth. He took a couple deep breaths and the nitrous oxide put him to sleep. The delicate surgery began at about 6:45 p.m. Dr. Seering first cleaned the area of any foreign matter. Squares, uneven rectangles, triangles, odd shapes, and all shapes of glass fragments were removed from Delloye's eye and scalp. One by one, each piece was placed in a metal bowl, cleaned, and dried. So he would never forget, Dr. Senn kept these shards of glass inside a safe; a kind gesture that he later shared with his patient.

"Okay, let's take a closer look" Dr. Seering muttered beneath his surgeon's mask as he examined Delloye's injured eye and left forearm.

The operative record nurse documented Dr. Seering's findings: "Left eyeball penetrated at the corner with leakage. Piece of glass, a half inch in diameter…slightly concave in eyeball in front of lens. Bullet entrance with funnel-like path above eyeball with lodgment of bullet in bones of skull above orbit. Bullet wounds above elbow caused by penetration of flesh pointing out to humerus about six-inch entrance to exit."

"Let's take care of the eye first, then the arm wounds." Dr. Seering requested the small delicate eyelid retractors used to spread and hold open the eyelids. Instrument nurse Fahey handed Dr. Seering the clamps, which were carefully fastened and clipped into place, one on the upper lid and one below. The bloodshot, bruised, and swollen eye stared at the ceiling. The pupils were fixed, motionless, and unresponsive to light. The globe hardly looked an eye. Red-purple with blood, it was both partly collapsed from the glass penetration yet the remaining tissue was swollen and bulging out of the socket.

"Scalpel. And have the sponges ready," directed Dr. Seering.

The doctor carefully trimmed away the conjunctiva and tenons fascia — the outer coats of the eye. Then the extraocular muscles, responsible for directing the eye toward what the brain wanted to see, were disconnected from the globe, and removed. Finally, the left optic nerves were cut and the entire eyeball was removed. Bleeding was controlled with careful cauterization. Any remaining blood and pus was soaked up with sterile gauze.

When all bleeding was controlled and the socket was dry, Dr. Seering carefully inserted an orbital implant deep in the socket and covered it with the conjunctiva, a pink tissue similar to the lining of the mouth. A temporary prosthetic conformer made of clear plastic was placed over the orbital implant. The conformer helped maintain the natural shape of the eye socket and lids. It would remain in for a couple weeks until the custom made prosthesis was available. To minimize swelling, a pressure patch was applied over the eyelids and secured with white pieces of tape. Finally, to help reduce pressure in the right eye, Brimonidine was given intravenously. Morphine was discontinued and codeine took its place.

Closely inspecting Delloye's left arm, the small entrance wounds and larger exit wounds, Dr. Seering confirmed what he first thought. The bullets had gone cleanly through, miraculously missing any tendons, arteries, and bones. He cleaned, disinfected, drained, and bandaged them. Anesthesia was stopped. The procedure, a success, took only thirty-two minutes. Delloye's gas mask was removed and he was taken to the recovery room, where he rested several hours while recovering from the nitrous oxide.

Dr. Seering removed his surgical mask and pulled off his gloves. He walked to the waiting room and sat alongside Mrs. Delloye. He gently placed a reassuring hand on her left shoulder and explained, "The operation went as planned. No complications. He will be a bit sore and might have trouble, temporarily, opening his right eye. This is normal and it will correct itself within 24 hours. I placed a pressure patch over his left eye socket that will keep the prosthetic eye in place and reduce swelling. The bullet behind his left eye will remain because it's too risky to remove. He's going to be in the hospital a few weeks yet. You are welcome to visit and be with him anytime. Do you have any questions for me?"

Clara Delloye took a deep breath and replied, "No, Doctor. Thank you so much."

"You're welcome," the doctor said. "God bless." He walked away as Mrs. Delloye watched his white coat round the corner and shrink out of sight.

Mrs. Delloye slowly walked towards Gus' room and imagined what he might look like. "My husband, with only one eye? Will I be able to take care of him? Will he be the same?" These were questions any loved one would ask when faced with the unknown.

She stood alongside her husband. Staring. The clean, white pressure patch cradled his left eye. His bandaged left arm rested, straight along his left side. His chest rose and fell slowly, yet peacefully. Dr. Seering's comments had been soothing and a sense of calm overcame her, but she realized that things were going to be different.

Thursday, July 23, 1931

Delloye's road to recovery was just beginning. Family, friends, and co-workers visited regularly. Every prayer and act of kindness helped. Clara Delloye had plenty of help around the house, which allowed her to spend considerable time with Gus.

Like anybody else with a bullet in their head, Delloye constantly complained of head pain and pressure. Ice bag after ice bag along with regular doses of codeine helped relieve it. But over time chronic pain would take its toll, both physically and emotionally. Delloye wouldn't even be able to sit up for another ten days.

The bandits had disappeared and the tips became less frequent. No cop every wants to admit it, especially to the general public, but it was evident they didn't have a clue who had done it. Speculation had many believing that Chicago gangsters were the ones. This was fueled by the report of the fleeing vehicle with an Illinois license plate along with the gangsters' style and technique. It was evident that these gangsters had some experience.

"Police Admit They Haven't a Single Clue in Bank Stickup" — Green Bay Press-Gazette

This first weekend following the robbery was eventful, but it fell short of cracking the case. The 72 hours of twists and turns began early Friday afternoon (July 24, 1931). Police received a tip about three suspicious Assyrians staying at a local hotel. Desperate for answers, police brought them to the station for questioning, but they were released a short time later. It was discovered that they were visiting the city to sell "fancy work" and didn't have any knowledge or involvement in the robbery.

Later that same evening, patrol Officer Frank Meert was visiting Delloye in the hospital. Meert parked his personal vehicle near the front of the hospital along S. Webster Avenue. Who would think his vehicle would be mistaken for a gas pump? Well, it was.

Three Michigan youths traveling through Green Bay on a "tour of the lakes" thought Meert's vehicle was parked just right for gasoline siphoning. They stopped along side his vehicle, carefully removed the gas tank cap, inserted the hose into both tanks, and began fuel transfer. However, their pit stop was suddenly interrupted.

"Can I help you boys?" Meert asked. Startled, these gas thieves didn't know what to do. Meert was happy to oblige. He promptly placed them under arrest. They were brought to the police department for questioning. With more important things to do, the thieves were lectured, released, and banished from the city. They promised to never return.

Saturday morning, July 25, 1931, started with a promising lead. Officers in Iowa City had arrested three men driving a red Auburn on some unrelated charges. Aware of the bank robbery, the Iowa City officers mailed the booking photos to Green Bay Police for possible eyewitness identification. The photos were shown to Slupinski, Cayer, Golden, and others with no luck. These were not Green Bay's most wanted.

Burke and others continued to work through the weekend. It allowed them to catch up, complete reports, and review what was known thus far. With limited physical evidence, no positive suspect identifications, and several eyewitness accounts, Burke had no choice but to rely solely on method of operation and brief suspect descriptions. He listed, studied, evaluated and analyzed what was known.

• Two vehicles used, described as a dark blue or black Nash with partial Illinois plate of "48," black Pierce Arrow, or a maroon Studebaker. One vehicle stopped in front of the bank while the other waited down the road.

• Five gangsters, all well dressed in double-breasted suits, unmasked, participated in the bank robbery and shoot out.

They used Tommy sub machine guns and revolvers. Seemed experienced. Two additional gangsters in the other vehicle acted as lookouts and helped with getaway — bringing the total number of gangsters involved to seven.

• Inside the bank, the gangsters seemed organized. They didn't waste any time and went right to the cash cages and vault. Two of them jumped the cages and cleared the vault while one stayed at the door. He appeared to be the leader. Employees were also controlled, rounded up, and roughly treated. They were ordered to lie on the floor and two male employees were struck on the head with the butt of a weapon.

• One gangster, the wounded one, described as a male, darker complexion — Italian looking, shorter, about five feet tall with a medium build. Other physical descriptions are incomplete and sketchy.

• Some of the other bandits may have also been shot, but didn't appear affected. They may have been wearing steel vests, which is common among experienced bank robbers.

• Evidence — several shell casings and bullet fragments; some have been turned over to the WBA and ABA for comparison. No fingerprints found inside the bank.

This method of operation was somewhat unique. He also realized that it was dumb luck, a fluke, that they had interrupted the robbery in progress. The gangsters and police were both caught off-guard. They would both learn from their mistakes. Burke also realized that his best chances of apprehending these gangsters would be when they struck again. Hopefully they wouldn't return to this city.

Monday, July 27, 1931

"Green Bay Police, Captain Burke," he answered the phone and hoped that this was the call that closed the case.

Again, it was the Appleton police and they now reported, "We got this guy in jail from Chicago, a church burglar, his name is John Frawley, claims to know who did your robbery. You might be interested in talking to him." Burke agreed and left just before the noon hour.

He arrived forty-five minutes later and sat across from Frawley, a seasoned fifty-four-year-old criminal, likely experienced at this game of cat and mouse. Burke wondered what Frawley's motive was for "chirping" about the robbery. Like all good detectives, Burke was armed with information about the robbery known only by police. Not everything was given to the media. A well-known technique used to filter out the "crackpots" that claim they did it or know who did. There were no offers on the table. They wouldn't talk about any sort of bargain until Frawley was done and his information checked out.

Burke sat back, listened, and took occasional notes. Knowing that writing down every word can cause one to become hesitant, he only noted the important points. A written statement, if needed, would be taken the second or third time through the interview.

Frawley alleged that a Green Bay man was involved in the robbery. Burke was taken back by this information and doubted its reliability. These gangsters were too experienced, organized, and well armed. It was not the job of some small time local boys.

Burke summed up his short interview with Frawley and told him, "You appear to be seeking some sympathy." Burke then slid back his chair, stood up, and walked out. He placed little stock in Frawley's statements and none of them could be verified.

Burke thanked the Appleton police for their assistance and headed back to Green Bay. It was a long, frustrating drive north. He continually thought about the case and began to realize the little hope there was left in "collaring" the gangsters. This wasn't right! People who shoot police officers are not supposed to escape the long arm of the law.

Tuesday, July 28, 1931

This early morning would generate the final tip. "Where to from here?" Burke wondered to himself. Any glimmer of hope, somebody in the right place at the right time, or maybe a guilty conscious would prevail and one of the gangsters would turn themselves in.

All reliable leads had pointed west until an interesting phone call was received from New Holstein, Wis., forty-five miles to the south. The sheriff reported, "We just got a call from a filling station of six men in a car, two of them apparently wounded, and they also had what looked like a machine gun."

Burke requested that all deputies in the area check for the vehicle. The sheriff assured him that it was already being done and followed with this interesting remark, "It appeared that the car was being driven by a woman." Burke noted this as well. Little did he know that this keen observation would be yet another piece of the puzzle.

The New Holstein vehicle was never located. If it had been involved, it was probably heading south towards Milwaukee or Chicago.

A Miraculous Recovery

Within two weeks of being critically wounded, Delloye went from near death to sitting up in bed, taking his first steps, and enjoying the company of those closest to him, his family. But it wouldn't be trouble free. His daily regiment consisted of sleep, wounds being cleaned and dressed, pain management, three square meals, a sponge bath, new white sheets and linens, entertain visitors, and more sleep. The head pain was the worst. It would bring him nearly to the breaking point. The piercing pain and pressure alone was too much for anybody to handle. But add losing an eye and possibly a career you love and these are the perfect ingredients for depression. Although Delloye was a true warrior, he was also human.

Twelve days into his new life he had enough and broke down. The pain had taken its toll. He wept and just wanted it to go away. He wanted his old life back. He wanted out of the hospital! He wanted to be home. He wanted everything to be normal.

Dr. Senn sat alongside Delloye and did the best he could to listen and reassure him that although his life wouldn't be exactly the same, he would adjust, survive, overcome, and adapt. Dr. Senn didn't say it would be easy, but like most police officers with a solid Type-A personality that doesn't quit, Delloye wouldn't give up. He also had the support of the police department behind him. Chief Hawley assured him that he would still and always be a police officer with the city of Green Bay. Most importantly, Delloye had the support of his family and the solid foundation of his faith. Faith, family, and friends are the ingredients that conquer depression and restore warriors. Delloye had those ingredients in their proper order. He eventually realized this and within a couple of hours his emotional condition improved.

Delloye continued to ride the rough road to recovery. He would improve a little bit each day. The wounds drained less and less as they continued to heal. He regained full use of his left arm. He learned to live with the pressure patch on his eye while waiting for his prosthetic one to arrive. His right eye didn't suffer any sympathetic inflammation and he had full use of it.

A New Eye on Life

Aug. 14, 1931, would be a somewhat momentous day in Delloye's life. Dr. Senn visited him at 8 a.m. bearing a gift. The prosthetic glass eye had arrived. It looked so real, an amazing resemblance to his right eye. The white yolk and brown iris were an exact match. The glass eye wasn't a perfect circle, but more like an odd-shaped kidney bean. Similar to the eye socket, it was round on the top, bottom, and outside with a gradual curve towards the center where it conformed to the nose. He wondered what it was going to feel like.

Dr. Senn took considerable time educating Delloye about his glass eye. To help the detective become more comfortable handling it, he was allowed to hold it in the palm of his hand while the procedures he would follow the rest of his life were explained.

"The eye should be cleaned at least once a day with luke-warm water. Do not use alcohol or any other harsh cleaners. Not only will it damage the eye, but it will also inflame your eye socket. Whenever you remove the eye, be sure your hands are clean. When showering, you can aim the spray directly into your eye. Just put your right hand over your right eye to prevent any discomfort from the direct spray."

Delloye listened intently and Dr. Senn explained how to insert the glass eye. "First of all, whenever you insert or re-move your glass eye, do it over a soft surface. You never know when you might fumble it." They chuckled at this lame bit of football humor. Dr. Senn proceeded, "You can moisten the eye a bit to make insertion easier. Begin by lifting up the upper eyelid with your left index finger and slightly pushing down your lower eyelid with your thumb. Holding the eye with your right index finger and thumb, push it under the lifted upper eyelid and then into the socket. It will slide right into place. If necessary, you can adjust the fit by touching the eye slightly and maneuvering it until it's comfortable. Sometimes air will get behind it and you can gently push it out." Dr. Senn also demonstrated this process.

Dr. Senn inserted it the first time for Delloye. It was a weird feeling — so cold, hard, and impersonal. But it soon became part of the detective's persona, something others would recognize him by. He adjusted and tried to become comfortable with his new eye while Dr. Senn explained the removal procedure.

"Remember, especially when removing the eye, make sure there is a soft surface below and be prepared to catch it. Also, make sure your hands are clean. To remove it, simply stand in front of a mirror and look upwards while at the same time place your left index finger in the middle of your lower eyelid and lashes. Pull the lower eyelid down until the edge of the eye is available. Apply inward pressure toward the inside corner of the eye and push toward the temple, almost like you are gouging it. It should begin to slip out of the cavity and be prepared to catch it." Dr. Senn also demonstrated this for Delloye and walked him through it. With a few rounds of practice, the detective got the hang of it.

Dr. Senn's final instructions were the most important. "If you ever need to rub your eye, do it in the direction of your nose. If you rub away from your nose and towards your temple, you might twist the eye or even accidentally press it out, which would surely lead to a fumble or incomplete pass."

These procedures were also shared with Clara Delloye. If for some reason her husband would be unable to, she had to also feel comfortable removing the eye. There was also an optional suction cup procedure that was explained. Simply put, a moistened suction cup could be used to rapidly pull it out of the socket.

It wouldn't take long for Delloye to become comfortable with the daily routine of his glass eye care regiment. Regular removal, cleansing, insertion, and adjustment soon became a way of life.

Exactly one month later would be Delloye's favorite day of this tragedy. He awoke on this Aug. 19, a pleasant summer morning, with high hopes. His arm wounds had completely healed. Much of the head pain and discomfort had subsided. He was comfortable with his glass eye. He was ready to go home.

Dr. Senn conducted one last exam and agreed; it was time for Delloye to leave. The discharge papers were prepared and explained. Much of it was a review for him. Delloye had become quite proficient and comfortable with his new way of life. With Mrs. Delloye by his side, he sat up, and with a quarter turn, his feet where on the floor. He stood up. Arm-in-arm, the Delloyes proudly walked out of room 103 and never looked back. It was a place that he was happy to leave. A waiting vehicle drove them home. There wouldn't be a big welcome home. Delloye didn't want it that way. The loving arms of his wife and children were enough. Ranging in age from five to twenty-two, Lucille, Margaret, Bernice, James, Lorraine, Roselind, and Laverne — their prayers were answered — papa was home.

Firm handshakes, hugs, and pats on the back. Fellow officers welcomed Delloye back at work on Sept. 1, 1931. They were glad to have him, but certain politicians felt differently. Some city council members argued that he was now disabled and unable to work at 100 percent. They estimated that he could still perform 75 percent of his duties and cut his salary by 25 percent. Delloye's objections fell on deaf ears. He was left with only one choice, hire legal counsel and take the city to court. He chose Green Bay attorney Clement W. Dwyer.

They filed a complaint with the Wisconsin Industrial Commission requesting that Delloye maintain his present salary and be reimbursed $5,019 for court costs, attorney's fees, pain and suffering. They won and the city still refused to pay. With the continued support of the police department behind them, Attorney Dwyer fired off an eloquent letter that not only appealed to logic, but emotions as well.

LAW OFFICES OF
DWYER & DWYER
MINIHAN BUILDING

Thos. C. Dwyer
Clement W. Dwyer
GREEN BAY, WIS

Dear Sir;
In re: August Delloye — Compensation

I believe it quite necessary that all interested parties concerning the governing of the police department be made acquainted with all the material facts concerning the August Delloye case…

Mr. Delloye entered employment of the Green Bay Police Department on May 1, 1916, at the time being a patrolman. He worked in this capacity until the spring of 1922 when he was promoted to the position of night desk sergeant. He worked in this capacity until the spring of 1924 when he was transferred to the plainclothes department as a detective. Later, in either 1926 or early in 1927, the office of Lieutenant in the plainclothes department was created and Mr. Delloye was promoted to this position, and this position he held at the time of his injury, which he still holds today.

It is interesting to note that from May 1, 1916, up to the present time he has never been cited either to his superior officers or the fire and police commission for being derelict in his duties. On the contrary, he has been cited on numerous occasions for valor and ability and in one year had the unusual record of singly making 96 arrests. As a matter of fact there is no officer presently employed who has a better record for service and conduct both on and off duty than Mr. Delloye…

Another interesting thing to note is that Officer Delloye has never availed himself of the time off, being one day out of each eight, nor has he availed himself of the vacation privileges accorded to other members of the department, and as a matter of fact on one occasion worked for ten months without taking off one single day, and as a matter of fact this year despite his disability, although entitled to a leave of one day in every eight, he has only taken off three days in a period of over six months. With the exception of Captain Burke, there is no other officer in the department who has put in more time toward his duties both in hours per day, days per week, and weeks per year, than August Delloye. In the whole period of his service in the department he was never off for sickness or vacation and the only time he lost was the period from July 20 to September 1 while he was recovering from the bullet wounds which caused the loss of his eye, part of the bullet being still embedded in his skull...

I submit this for your careful consideration and respectfully submit that August Delloye be retained in the employ of the city until disqualified or removed for proper cause, and that the city immediately pay to him the award set forth by the Industrial Commission.

Respectfully submitted,
Clement W. Dwyer
CWD: EK

Like many tragedies, as time goes on many forget the sacrifices. Delloye had nearly died for his city. He never thought of early retirement or going out on disability, which he could have easily done. He was a cop and nobody was going to take that away from him! Delloye won this battle, too. Although he would no longer be a detective, he was assigned night shift commander, a job like all others that he performed with dedication and pride. Perseverance — that was exemplified by August Delloye.

Burke continued to be the lead investigator, but all members of the department, officers and detectives alike worked the case, which had reached a dead end. The gangsters committed a "Houdini" — they had vanished without a trace.

Within a couple of months, the Green Bay Police Department was the recipient of their very own Tommy submachine gun. A local bankers' association donated three Tommy guns, two to the sheriff's department and one to the police department. They wouldn't be outgunned again.

October 19, 1931 — Somewhere in St. Paul, Minnesota

The bandits prepared for their next take. A little pep talk helped maintain the gangsters' courage and will. One gangster, the leader, spoke up. "Green Bay was a farce. Those cops got lucky. Next time it won't be so pretty. Tomorrow we hit the Kraft State Bank in tiny Menominee. Four of us will work the bank and two of you will wait down the road. Deal with any trouble. Be careful driving through the crooked bridges over the border. The cops work those roads."

Tuesday, October 20, 1931 — Kraft State Bank, Menominee, Wisconsin

It was another great day for a bank robbery. The weather was perfect, not too cold, just right for these bandits dressed in their double-breasted suits concealing body armor, Tommy guns, and revolvers.

Four bandits occupied the large black Lincoln sedan, with Minnesota license plate B361-500. An experienced military-trained machine gunner and former elected sheriff gone bad, drove and manned his Tommy gun. They rolled into Menominee at about 9 a.m. The sedan stopped along the sidewalk a short half-block away from the target. A second getaway car, a gray coupe, blended into the area, but was later recognized by a mail carrier.

Three gangsters exited and casually walked toward the Kraft State Bank. Their suit coats helped them blend into the environment. The driver kept the motor running, prepared for a quick escape. They entered the bank and wasted no time getting started. Well planned, well armed, and experienced, it was to be another easy take.

R. A. Rommelyer, assistant cashier, watched the first

gangster slowly stroll up to his counter. The short, stocky thug, wearing a gray suit and no hat, seemed like the typical customer. Rommelyer, instead of beginning his routine "How can I help you" greeting, was met with a sobering order. "Get down on the floor!" demanded the gangster. Rommelyer, now staring down the barrel of a Tommy gun, wasted no time complying. This gangster remained near the front of the bank and appeared to be the leader. The two other machine-gun-toting accomplices executed their mission.

The second gangster entered the office of James Kraft, the owner's son, and ordered him to the floor as well. Kraft immediately complied. Satisfied, the gangster strolled to the back of the bank and greeted five other employees with a cheery, "Good morning everybody. Come out here and lie down." All of them complied. Nobody offered any resistance. He could now monitor several compliant employees and a few customers who were face down near the center of the bank.

The third gangster had made his way behind the cash cages and ordered Assistant Cashier William Kraft to open the safe. Quickly, he rotated the dial and opened it. He was then ordered to the floor and found himself on his stomach only a few feet away from the open vault.

Take it easy, we've got plenty of time," the gangster at the door shouted. $2,973 in cash, $87,000 in registered bonds, and $7,940 in negotiable bonds were stuffed into bags they had brought with them. Little did the bandits realize, the registered bonds were useless and couldn't be cashed without bank authorization.

Holy shit! Vernon Townsend thought to himself while he witnessed the bank robbery from his bulletproof cage on the raised balcony near the back. The armed guard did what he was trained to do. He sounded the alarm and quickly found his way to the rooftop where he hoped to get a chance to shoot at the fleeing bandits.

The ringing alarm made it known to everybody inside that

the police and armed posses were on their way. Unlike the Green Bay robbery, this allowed the gangsters to formulate a quick escape plan.

"Where's the rest of the dough?" the unsatisfied gangster snarled towards William Kraft from inside the vault.

"That's all there is," Kraft replied.

"It's not enough! We want more! Kick in quick!" the bandit demanded while walking up to craft and kicking him in the head.

"Kill him if he doesn't tell!" said another.

Pleading, Kraft tried to assure them. "I'm not lying. You've got all there is."

"To hell with you!" The cold-blooded criminal squeezed the trigger. The bullet spun out of the barrel and drilled its way into Kraft's left shoulder, shattering bone and tearing soft tissue. The bullet continued through his body, pierced a lung, exited just above the heart, and embedded itself in the wooden floor.

"Let's get out of here…"

The action outside the bank had already begun. Alert citizens, believing the Lincoln sedan to be suspicious, took it upon themselves to investigate. An armed vigilante tried to get a closer look but was met with a blast of Tommy submachine gun fire. Bullets shattered windows and splintered wood siding in businesses across the street. About the same time, the alarm went off and the Lincoln slowly drove forward and parked in the middle of the road in front of the bank.

The driver exited with his Tommy gun in hand. He scanned forward, backward, and side-to-side, sweeping his machine gun toward the crowds of onlookers and any armed vigilantes who might be thinking of taking a shot. Just to make sure, he fired a few warning shots above their heads.

Back inside the bank, the three bandits hurriedly planned their escape. Expecting resistance, they used human shields to lessen the chances of being shot.

"You! Get up! Get up!" one bandit shouted at James Kraft. Kraft complied and rose to his feet. The bandit grabbed Kraft by the back of the neck and escorted him toward the door. Another bandit grabbed a terrified female employee and told her, "Your going out with us," while walking her towards the door. Failing to comply was not an option. With their shields in hand, all three bandits emerged from the bank hiding behind Kraft and Schafer. Schafer stumbled and fell to the sidewalk, which allowed her to escape and run off. They maintained control of Kraft and shoved him into the awaiting car.

All the gangsters piled in and the car began to speed off. From his elevated vantage point, armed guard Townsend opened fire on the back of the fleeing machine. Several armed citizens joined in and also shot at the bandits. Bullets shattered the rear and front windows. Tommy gun fire was returned and sprayed the streets in front of and around the bank.

"Arrrgh! I'm shot!" cried one of the bandits. A vigilante's bullet had found its mark and speared a gangster's eye.

The chase was on. The gangsters had a considerable head-start. They had planned their getaway well and sprinkled nails on the road to prevent successful pursuit. The armed posse chased but couldn't catch up.

About six miles north of town the Lincoln came to a halt. "You're not gonna make it, pal," one gangster told his wounded comrade. They dragged him out, laid him in the ditch with his revolvers, and left some money on his chest just in case he survived. His steel vest failed him and had been penetrated by a vigilante's bullet. There was another round in his head that had entered his right eye. He died a short time later and was identified as Frank Webber.

To avenge Webber's death, a round was placed in the back of 19-year-old James Kraft's head. His body was dumped near Webber's. The surviving gangsters sped off due north and then west toward Minnesota.

Not all was well. Another bandit was wounded, shot through the neck and left knee. Both wounds were not immediately fatal and it would take several hours for him to die. He laid in the back seat in agonizing pain. If that wasn't enough, just when they thought they were home free in Webb Lake, Wis., near the Minnesota border (100 miles north of Menomonie), their successful escape was interrupted by road construction.

"Damn it! We're stuck," mumbled the driver. They found their wheels spinning in a rut on a road under construction. Thankfully, there was a road crew willing to help them get underway. Even though the driver was bleeding from the mouth and another person lay in the back seat covered with a blanket, the road crew was happy to oblige. They gathered around the back of the machine and pushed the gangsters on their way. They were impressed with the Wisconsin hospitality. Until then, bandits could only find similar customer service in St. Paul, the gangster's paradise.

A few miles later, the second wounded gangster became extra baggage. He also died and was given a gangster's burial. His body was tossed in a ditch along with the tools of his trade, a Tommy gun and pistol. Fingerprint records identified him as ex-Leavenworth convict Charles Preston Harmon.

The surviving two gangsters fled into Minnesota, burned their car in a farmer's field near Cambridge, and found their way home to St. Paul.

Twenty-two-year-old William Kraft survived the gunshot wound. Mourning the death of the younger Kraft brother, the citizens of Menomonie were angered and demanded justice.

The bodies of Webber and Harmon were brought back to Menomonie. None of their family members or relatives came forward to claim the corpses. The citizens of Menomonie provided an appropriate burial place, the Potter's field, which was shared by deceased members of the asylum. They were dumped, one on top of the other, in a single plot and buried. Steel rods, like the ones used to enclose jail cells, were fashioned into a cross and shoved into the ground at the head of their eternal resting place.

The investigation into the identities of the surviving bandits continued for several months. With the assistance of the Minnesota Bureau of Criminal Apprehension, two of the bandits were eventually identified as Francis Keating and Tommy Holden. Warrants were issued for their arrest. Keating and Holden, escapees who had been serving time for a 1928 mail robbery in Evergreen Park, Ill., were affectionately known as the Green River Bandits. Menomonie authorities would patiently await their apprehension and then notify the Green Bay Police.

"Think Menomonie Bandits Robbed South Side Bank" — *Green Bay Presss-Gazette, October 22, 1931*

The all-points bulletin had been received at the Green Bay Police Department. "Gus! Gus!" shouted Captain Burke. "Looks like our bank robbers struck again in Menomonie."

This bank robbery had also made headline news throughout the state. The police read the newspaper and began to note the eerie similarities between both jobs. The methods of operation and bandit descriptions matched. It's no secret that bandits, like all people, are creatures of habit and replicate behaviors that get results. These bank robbers were no different; they used their techniques that worked, both in Menomonie and Green Bay.

The names of Webber and Harmon were noted. Burke got on the phone with Menomonie and requested photographs and fingerprint records on both. Menomonie police promised to send them ASAP. Burke questioned them about the robbery and noted additional similarities. He later told the Green Bay media, "The robbers who succeeded in the daylight robbery of the South Side State Bank also wore steel vests as they were shot at directly and apparently hit without injury. This alone, however, is insufficient cause for believing the two gangs are the same because nearly all of the bank robbing gangs are so equipped."

However, the similarities were much deeper then that and Burke and Delloye knew it. They had a strong circumstantial case based upon a unique method of operation.

They would have to patiently await photographs of Webber and Harmon and hope for positive witness identification. Once received, their photos would be shown around town and hotel records checked to see if they had stayed in the area. Even if they had, they likely registered under false names and couldn't be traced. Green Bay Police also anxiously awaited news of the arrests of Keating and Holden and to get a shot at interrogating them as well.

In exchange for Delloye's left eye, a sort of vengeance had been dealt to Webber and Harmon. Delloye shared this exciting news with his family and he hoped to see the other two gangsters responsible for his pain and suffering in the near future. Sadly, that day would never come.

"Retiring Chief Feted at Dinner" — *Green Bay Press-Gazette, June 3, 1946*

Chief Hawley led his department through this tragedy and many others for the next fifteen years. He wouldn't retire until May 31, 1946, after 53 years of service including 49 of them as chief of police. His length of service set a record for police chiefs in the state and potentially the nation. Over 300 people from all walks of life celebrated his retirement. Ordinary citizens, chiefs of police throughout the Midwest, FBI agents, and other law enforcement professionals honored this leader. A personal letter of recognition was also sent from J. Edgar Hoover, head of the FBI.

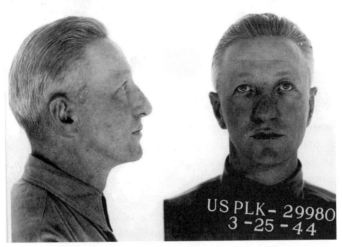

A booking photo of Francis L. "Jimmy" Keating, a suspect in the South Side Bank Robbery. (Photo courtesy of the National Archives - Pacific Region, San Francisco.)

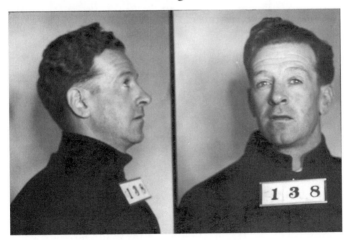

A booking photo of Thomas Holden, who escaped with Jimmy Keating and was a suspect in the South Side Bank Robbery. (Photo courtesy of the National Archives - Pacific Region, San Francisco.)

Keynote speaker Harry T. O'Connor, chief agent in charge of the Cleveland FBI office, best described the true impact of Hawley's legacy. "It is impossible to evaluate the contribution that Tom Hawley has made to the well-being of this community. He has brought to his profession a set of high ideals which have had an incalculable influence for good, not only upon the men immediately around him in his own profession, but upon men in all occupations — as the representation at this banquet proves. For more than half a century this public official, prominently placed in his community, has radiated goodness, justice, and integrity." Hawley left his mark and the incoming chief had some big shoes to fill.

Hawley retired to his modest home at 514 Kellogg Street on the city's near west side. His plan? To spend much needed time with the love of his life, his wife. But his well-deserved rest and recuperation wouldn't last more than five years. On March 22, 1951, Hawley died of a broken heart. A few months earlier, he lost his wife to illness followed by the death of his brother, who was killed in a car accident. These factors were believed to have contributed to the breakdown in his health. At the age of 84, this legend was laid to rest in Fort Howard Cemetery surrounded by those family members who had preceded him.

"Lt. Delloye Ends Four Decades in Police Department" - *Green Bay Press-Gazette, May 1, 1956*

Lt. August Delloye would never see the gangsters that changed his life brought to justice. Delloye went on to complete forty years of service with the Green Bay Police Department, retiring as the night shift lieutenant at the age of 70. Many in his same position today would have retired on disability, but this warrior carried on and served his city well.

As the years passed, Delloye wouldn't talk much about the

robbery. If somebody asked, he would share bits and pieces. However, the story was never complete and justice never served. Although the bank robbery changed his appearance, it didn't change the person or the police officer he was inside.

Delloye not only served his city, but was also dedicated to his family. It was his long standing daily routine to finish his night shift, come home and tend to his large garden in the backyard with the serenading songs of the morning birds, place some fresh food on the kitchen counter for the family, give his wife a hug and a kiss and finally go to bed.

Delloye took such pride in his garden that he would sometimes go to great lengths to spruce it up a bit. Any little addition to it was a bonus. For example, a few years prior to the bank robbery, while walking his Main Street beat during the early morning hours, he came across a large wooden barrel in the middle of the street. Not only was this barrel a potential traffic hazard, it would be a great addition to his garden. The wooden 50-gallon barrel with metal straps around the top, center, and bottom would easily hold a load of topsoil. Figuring that it fell off a truck, Delloye knew it was his civic duty to take action. After all, it was winter, the roads could get slick, and somebody might slam on their brakes to avoid it and crash. Delloye couldn't live with that. He looked left and right before entering the road, quickly pranced to the barrel and wrapped his arms around it. Bear hugging it, Delloye scooted back to the sidewalk and behind a Main Street business where he set it in the alley. This little workout wasn't enough for Delloye to warm up from the winter cold and he made his way to the Main Street fire station. Once inside, Delloye began to heat up and so did the awful substance that was now coming from his stained and soiled uniform. "What is that awful smell?" Delloye murmured to himself. "Why do I smell like crap?" Delloye soon answered his own question when he realized that it was a very special barrel that he had just made his own. Turns out that it had fallen off of an outhouse truck and was stained, both inside and out, with human feces and urine, which now covered the front of his uniform. Needless to say, the barrel never made it home, but Delloye sure did that same night to change into a new uniform.

Delloye enjoyed telling these stories of the days gone by. The ones that made him and others laugh were preferred. When not telling stories and work had to be done, he was a serious and caring night shift commander. When asked, Delloye was always willing to indirectly offer advice or answer a law enforcement related question. His answers were always prefaced with, "My boy, if it were me, this is what I would do…" If you had the time and listened closely he would always provide the right answer.

Also known to be quite frugal, it was common knowledge to never open a pack of cigarettes in front of Delloye because he would dump them out and take half. He also loved Al's Hamburgers,* fried fresh downtown on South Adams Street, and could smell the odor permeating from the uniforms of officers who had just left there and returned to the station. To the hamburger toting officer Delloye would often say, "My boy, the next time you go to Al's, bring me one of those burgers, will ya?" New officers were happy to oblige until they soon learned that Delloye would never pay them back. In the end, it was said that he had so much money in his police credit union savings account that if he had withdrawn it all when he retired the credit union would have closed its doors.

Al's Hamburgers, 131 S. Washington St., remains today and still makes the finest hamburgers in the city.

Delloye was also a stickler for details and would have pen and paper in hand before answering the ringing night shift phone. He wrote down every detail and would get so engrossed in his work that the slightest sudden movement would make him flinch. The night and afternoon shift officers were well aware of this and played the occasional practical joke. Draping a fake spider tied to a length of chain in front of him while he was on the phone to watch him jump back and throw the receiver at it was the most common one. However, the dead flying bat was most memorable.

Afternoon shift officers found a dead bat and couldn't just throw it away; what a waste that would be. With the creative assistance of the night shift, they nailed the bat to a board and mounted it above the molding at the top of the wall facing Delloye's desk. For maximum effect, they pinned its wings open and tied a string around its neck. The string ran along the top of the wall into an adjoining room and when released the bat would fly right at him. Shortly after the shift started, an officer in the next room placed a fictitious phone call and with writing implements in hand Delloye answered it. The night shift officers watched from a few feet away as the bat soared at his head. "Jesus Christ!" Delloye yelled and threw the receiver at the bat. The receiver flew across the room and with a loud clang bounced off a metal gun cabinet.

The officers laughed their asses off and so did Delloye. But he had a difficult time getting over the fact that because of the prank, he missed a call from a deserving citizen. Nobody bothered to tell him that the phone call was also part of the gag.

Practical jokes were so common that afternoon shift officers would usually come in a half-hour before the end of their shift to participate in or just watch. When a joke wasn't played, Delloye thought there was something wrong. It was a love / hate thing. He refered to the pranksters as "gosh damn assholes," but at the same time laugh right along with them.

Delloye was respected by all of the officers that worked for him. He never forgot where he came from. He knew what it was like to walk the streets and risk his life. He valued his employees and they valued him. When he told them to do something they did it, no matter how crazy it might have seemed at the time. Not only would Delloye get the facts, he helped people in anyway he could, or had others help at his direction. Two occasions of "Delloye style" hospitality make this quite evident.

In the early 1950s a middle-aged overweight woman walked into the police department. She had been in a fight. Her hair was amiss, face scratched up, and blouse was torn with her right breast hanging out. Delloye didn't miss a beat. He grabbed his writing implements and was ready for her story. But first, he saw to it that she was "cleaned up a bit."

"My boy, my boy" Delloye said to the radio room officer. "Come here, take this lady into the radio room and fix her up a bit." A little hesitant, the officer wondered how the heck he was going to help a woman get her breast back in place. But he did and afterward Delloye did what he did best and took her complaint.

"Fish Eye" Lament walked into the night shift lobby a short time later. "Fish Eye" was well known in the city. His nickname came from his appearance. One eye was fake and the skin around it sagged from an ill-fitted glass eye. He was a regular who liked to drink a little too much and then get into a fight or two. On this particular night, he lost the fight and not only was he a bit bloody, he stood in front of Delloye holding his glass eye. Again, Delloye summoned the radio room officer. "My boy, my boy, take 'ol Fish Eye into the radio room and clean him up a bit." The officer complied and surely wished it were another breast he could handle instead of this eye. A breast is a bit easier to tuck away then inserting a glass eye. However, Fish Eye became yet another satisfied customer.

Delloye's legacy was not only known inside the police department, but outside too. From the streets of Green Bay to Racine, the bums knew him well. Delloye loved people, but disliked drunks. His signature send off of, "Throw his ass downstairs" was directed at the uncooperative vagrant who quickly found himself in a cell below.

When working the streets, Delloye knew how to play the game, when to give a break and when to be firm, but fair. He knew the letter of the law, but also understood the spirit of it, too. People respected and remembered him for that. For example, a panhandling bum in Racine sent his "hellos" to Delloye when he made the mistake of asking a visiting Green Bay police officer for some spare change.

"Don't be panhandling me," said the officer, identifying himself as one of one Green Bay's finest.

The bum replied, "How is good 'ol Gus Delloye doing? Say hello to him for me." Amazed, the officer couldn't believe that somebody, a lowly bum 150 miles south of Green Bay knew Delloye.

Delloye also knew when to be creative and it saved his life more than once. His attention to detail in all aspects of his job not only helped him thoroughly document the facts, but also helped solve many crimes, too. On his beat, he even noticed the slightest cobweb that was out of place. One night, while checking the back door of a business, he noticed just that. A cobweb in the upper corner, which had been present the night before was gone. Somebody could have cleaned it, but that was unlikely. Delloye pulled on the door and found it opened. Could somebody be inside? Had they already pulled off the burglary and left? Delloye couldn't call for back up, he didn't have a radio. It was just himself and possibly the thief still at work. Delloye made a convincing and dynamic entry. He yelled, "You two in the front, two in the back, I'm going in." With the building now "surrounded" Delloye drew his weapon, swung open the back door, fired off a convincing warning shot into the air, and rapidly entered the building. "Don't shoot! Gus, don't shoot! The burglar pleaded as he popped his head up from behind the cash register. Delloye made the arrest and yet another case was closed.

Delloye was awarded several commendations. In his first

two years alone he single handedly interrupted five burglaries in progress and apprehended the suspects, recovered a murder weapon found on a Greenleaf, Wis., man he arrested who had shot his wife early the same day, and stopped three suspicious men with suitcases filled with stolen merchandise from a Menominee, Wis., burglary. The number of commendations became so numerous that the chief ran out of room on Delloye's department "History Card" that he finally noted, "Space is limited, for more important arrests, records on file at courthouse."

On October 18, 1956, the Fort Howard Chapter of the Military Order of the Purple Heart presented Delloye with an award for meritorious service. Shot twice in the line of duty, it was well deserved. Sadly, the police department never awarded Delloye with the appropriate Medal of Valor for "extraordinary heroism" in the line of duty. Gus Delloye, the warrior, police officer, father, and grandfather remained in the City of Green Bay and passed away peacefully on July 9, 1964. His memories of the Cannard extortion case and the South Side State Bank robbery died with him.

DeNamur and Burke went onto finish their careers with the Green Bay Police Department. Burke retired in 1936, five years after the robbery, completing 37 years of service with the department. The informal records division was officially closed. DeNamur completed his 22 years of service, retiring one year before Hawley. He was one of a few police officers that served the dual role of beat cop and department auto mechanic. These positions would later be split, one held by a sworn officer the other by a civilian auto repairman.

"Leavenworth Men Caught at Kansas City Golf Course..."
Associated Press, July 7, 1932

Just like the lives of Delloye, Hawley, DeNamur, and Burke faded into the past, so did this cold case. We will never be able to prove beyond a reasonable doubt if Francis Keating or Tommy Holden were involved in the South Side State Bank Robbery. The physical evidence, police reports, and the suspects themselves are gone. However, Keating and Holden probably did do it, and it is just that, Probable cause, which is needed to make an arrest.

Probable cause is defined as the quantum of evidence that would lead a reasonable police officer to believe that the suspect has committed or is committing a serious crime.

The Green Bay Police suspected that the same bandits who committed the Menominee bank robbery were also responsible for the South Side State Bank robbery. However, they didn't realize the great extent of probable cause and circumstantial evidence that they had. Due to poor communications along with a lack of adequate information sharing and resources, Detectives Burke and Delloye were denied significant pieces of information to help solve the puzzle.

Until now, this case was never completely revisited. The last documented news account dedicated to this robbery was on May 14, 1985. *Green Bay Press-Gazette* reporter Lois Kerin interviewed Bea Smits (former bank teller Bea Sager) and wrote about her terrifying account of this incident. The article speculated that John Dillinger's gang might have been responsible for the robbery.

The Dillinger theory makes perfect sense. He was a successful, experienced, and ruthless bank robber. His methods would definitely fit the profile. He robbed at least 10 banks in Indiana, Ohio, Wisconsin, and South Dakota. He was also a frequent visitor to this state, often traveling to the Green Bay area to visit his local girl, Evelyn Frechette, who spent time at Red Blacks Tavern, right next to the South Side State Bank. Dillinger also spent time further north at Little Bohemia resort in Manitowish Waters, Wis., 240 miles northwest of the city. Better yet, the alias name that he gave to Tucson police in 1934 was, "Frank Sullivan of Green Bay." He definitely had connections to Titletown.

However, there is a slight problem with the Dillinger theory. He had a solid alibi. He was in prison throughout 1931 and wouldn't begin his infamous bank robbing until 1934. It's rumored that federal agents questioned him sometime between 1933 and 1934 about the Green Bay robbery and he denied it stating something like, "That one was too small for me." If this did happen, it was a rare moment of honesty for Mr. Dillinger.

Other famous gangsters' names have come up as potential suspects. The infamous Al Capone and a former business partner, "Polack" Joe Saltis have both been considered suspects as well. Desperate for answers, these names are nothing more than mere speculation, not grounded on any solid evidence.

A brief study of Capone and Saltis quickly reveals that they were not bank robbers themselves. Capone likely associated with bank robbers. But his main business was racketeering, running rum along with his underground casinos, strip clubs, and brothels. Capone didn't rob banks, but rather made it his habit to eliminate the competition through murder and extortion. He frequented Wisconsin and would often travel to his favorite northern woods hideout in Couderay, Wis., for some much needed R&R. Even mobsters needed a vacation. His hideout was complete with a machine gun nest protecting the entrance. Even though he was prepared for it, Capone didn't come here to cause trouble, but rather lay low, relax, and stay away from the authorities.

In June of 1931, Capone was indicted for tax evasion, and spent his summer at his Lansing, Mich., hideout preparing his defense. He was convicted in October and sentenced to eleven years in prison.

Saltis, like Capone, was also a rumrunner. A Capone business partner, until he was discovered doing business with the competition, broke away and went out on his own. Saltis was a successful saloonkeeper and bootlegger on Chicago's southeast side. That was Saltis' niche and bank robbery wasn't his game. He frequented Wisconsin as well and often stayed at a cabin in Shawano, Wis., a mere 30 miles west of Green Bay. This was another gangster's getaway and he, too, didn't want to bring himself any attention. Saltis later invested $100,000 in Winter, Wis., where he built his retirement home.

Our focus then returns to the primary suspects, Keating and Holden. Who were these "Green River Bandits"? Where did they come from? What were their methods of operation? What other banks did they terrorize and rob?

Francis L. Keating, who preferred to be called Jimmy instead, was born in Chicago in 1899. When Keating was just seven years old, his father died and his mother raised him. Keating seemed to adjust well enough and knew what it was like to work hard and earn a living. He dropped out of school after eighth grade and labored to help make ends meet. He served his country in the U.S. Navy and upon his return he married a young lady named Alice. They settled in Chicago, had two sons, and appeared to be living the American dream. This all changed when Keating met his future partner in crime, Thomas Holden.

Holden, a good talker who sometimes put his skills to work as a self-titled car salesman, laborer, or steamfitter, was also born in Chicago. Dropping out of school in the sixth grade, Holden managed to live a stable childhood and married young to a girl, whose family members were well known to police and more or less trouble on account of law violations. While in his twenties, Holden was arrested on many occasions by the police, but had always succeeded in avoiding conviction. He later became known to the FBI as a dangerous criminal who was suspected to have taken part in some of the numerous major hold-ups in the Chicago area.

In February of 1928, an honest living became something of the past for Keating and Holden's luck ran out when they decided to pull a mail train robbery in Evergreen Park, Ill. It was a success! They made off with $135,000 and didn't plan on working another day. However, their new business venture was short-lived when they were apprehended several days later. Guilty of the offense, Keating and Holden began their 25 year sentence and arrived at Leavenworth on May 5, 1928.

Keating, now 29 years old, was a tough-looking fellow. Not real tall, only 5 feet 6 inches, his muscular build and six gold teeth that lined his upper front jaw made up for his lack of height. His baby face appearance said "trust me," but his actions spoke otherwise.

Holden, a couple years older, and a few inches taller, was slender with dark brown hair and a medium complexion. Thin faced, when reading, glasses sat on the bridge of his nose and his hair that naturally parted right accented his long forehead. His chin protruded from his long face and his piercing look could cause even an experienced inmate to swallow hard. When nervous or in deep thought, like when planning his escape, he constantly drew his lips tightly over his teeth.

Keating and Holden appeared to be model prisoners. In their first 18 months of incarceration, they both earned 3,000 days of good time. Their behavior was merely a mask for what they were really hoping to do — escape.

While inside the walls, they both befriended the infamous George "Machine Gun Kelly" Barnes and convicted murderer and bank robber Frank Nash. Keating and Holden were attracted to the bank robbery lifestyle. The excitement, the nightlife, and plenty of money couldn't be found inside the coop. These experienced criminals would be their ticket out.

Barnes had been serving time in Leavenworth on a bootlegging charge and was put to work in the records room where the measurements, fingerprints, and photographs of the inmates were kept. Utilizing Barnes' skills and knowledge, along with the assistance of Nash, they conjured up a clever escape plan. Through careful observation, Keating and Holden noted that on a daily basis trustees were let out of the south gate to work on the prison farm. Each trustee carried a picture identification card with his name on it. Barnes made the two men the needed identification cards and on February 28, 1930, when a replacement guard was working the gate, they walked out to their "farm detail" with no intention of ever coming back. Someday they would pay back Barnes. He told them if they ever needed anything on the outside to look them up or their good friend John Harvey Bailey (AKA Tom Brennan).

With smuggled-in civilian clothes worn underneath their prison garb, Keating and Holden dropped their Leavenworth stripes, ripped up their falsified passes, and walked away from the fields. They officially became FBI "Wanted Escaped Convicts" and this marked the beginning of their rein of terror throughout the Midwest.

Keating and his wife, along with Holden both set up shop in St. Paul, Minn. Once established, Holden then went to Minocqua, Wis., to join his wife, Lillian. She had been living there with relatives while Holden was serving his time. They then returned to their Minnesota flat.

Keating and Holden didn't waste much time getting involved in the bank robbery trade. Before entering prison, they had both been acquainted with "America's Most Successful Bank Robber," John Harvey Bailey. Unable to practice their trade while sitting in prison, they needed to work off some rust. Through Chicago connections, word had reached Bailey, who was now living in Kenosha County, Wis., that Keating and Holden were looking for him. They soon connected and it didn't take the two men long to begin their rehabilitation program and enroll in Bailey's "Bank Robbery 101" refresher course.

Bailey didn't become a bank robber extraordinaire overnight. He put in his time and earned his title. Missouri born, Bailey began his bank-robbing career in 1921 pulling off a nighttime robbery in Shenandoah, Iowa, that almost got him killed. While fleeing the bank with the loot, he and his companions were shot at by vigilantes concealed in the dark. Although frustrated, Bailey wasn't deterred, he just promised himself never to do another robbery under the moonlight. Logically, if you are going to pull off a robbery where shooting might take place, it's better to see the shooter while being shot at.

Before Bailey pulled off his first daylight robbery, he came up with a playbook that he followed with success time and again. First, all good honest bandits have to look the part. It's better to blend into the environment and maintain the element of surprise. Bailey would wear a respectable double-breasted suit, matching pants, and sometimes a straw-brimmed hat. It was perfect, a bank robber who looked like a banker. Bailey required this dress for all of his fellow bandits. If you didn't look the part, you didn't play the game.

Second, bandits needed wheels. If you could buy a car, great, if not just steal it. If purchased, it was always registered under a false name. Ideally, a second vehicle was also needed to serve as a lookout and to help with the getaway. The same rules that applied to the first vehicle applied to the second one too.

Third, any bank robber worth his salt needed a reliable gun. Bailey preferred his trusty .45-caliber revolver, but on occasion used the powerful Tommy gun. Heavy and cumbersome, but yet powerful and intimidating, the Tommy gun was a necessity that was usually carried by the man stationed at the door or with the vehicle parked in front of the bank. Any armed resistance could be effectively dealt with by the Tommy gun. Sawed-off shotguns were also acceptable options, both inside and outside the bank.

Fourth, all bank robberies had to be well planned, especially the getaway, which could be the most difficult part. The planning began days before the robbery and the leader(s) had to be confident in its success. Bailey would personally visit the target; note the time, the number of employees working, the building layout, and if it had an alarm. He would also learn the lay of the land and even contact the local surveyor's office and order maps of the county. Knowing that police would focus on main intersections, Bailey mastered the back roads, logging the distance and landmarks from one turn to the next. In order to confirm he got it right, Bailey then sent two trusted accomplices into the area to analyze and fine-tune the plans to make sure nothing was overlooked. These precise instructions were then written down and kept in the glove box for any bandit to reference. All other instructions were done by word of mouth only and on a need to know basis. Married bandits need not tell their wives.

Fifth, a few casualties were expected in this line of business and no wounded or dead bandit was worth getting jailed over. Severely wounded or dead bandits were considered a liability. They would be treated to the best of their abilities or until a trusted doctor could work on them. Dead or dying bandits would be dumped, normally alongside a road, while the remaining accomplices continued their escape.

Finally, before police had stop sticks or spike strips, Bailey came up with his own and less costly alternative. Costing less then a penny each, large headed roofing nails, sprinkled on the road were often used to flatten the tires of any pursuers. This is the curriculum that Holden and Keating were exposed to shortly after their escape. Now it was time to put it into practice.

Keating and Holden's first successful bank robbery took place on July 15, 1930. With the help of Bailey, "Machine Gun Kelly" Barnes, and two other experienced accomplices, Verne Miller and Sammy Silvermen, they staged a daring daylight robbery that began sometime between 10:15 and 10:30 a.m. Other accounts indicate that Robert "Frisco

Dutch" Steinhardt of Chicago also participated.

Well-dressed (easily mistaken for businessmen) and armed with Tommy guns and automatic pistols, they entered the Bank of Willmar, in the small Minnesota town with the same name. The machine gunner waited outside at the door, near the stolen getaway vehicle with Minnesota plates, while the remaining four went to work inside.

Methodically, they quickly had everyone inside either lying on the floor or standing with arms raised. Those who didn't immediately obey or move fast enough found a gun stuck into their belly, were shoved, or even kicked. Only the employees were treated like this and obedient customers were not harmed. The bandits leisurely took their time scooping up cash, securities, and gold from the cages and vault, which was opened by an employee at gunpoint.

The machine gunner outside kept citizens at bay and it was hoped that his show of force would prevent any armed vigilante resistance. It worked at first until two armed citizens took "pot shots" at the bandit and hit him. He returned fire into the crowds of innocent bystanders while his fellow gangsters exited with two employees being used as shields. The gangsters joined the shoot out, which allowed the human shields to escape to safety.

Indiscriminate bullets wounded two citizens, a mother and child, and the bandits blazed out of Willmar under a hail of gunfire. A second getaway vehicle driven by a female also followed them. Just to show their true disdain for the law, on their way out of town they fired a few rounds at the nearby courthouse. Since murder and bank robbery both carried a life sentence, a little thing like a human life meant nothing to them.

Witnesses described the leader of the gang, probably Keating, as a short, swarthy (e.g. Italian looking) complexioned man, with light suit and straw hat. He was every inch a desperate man, wielding a high-caliber gun, and brutally kicking those who dared to raise their heads. While the gangsters gathered their loot, Keating walked about covering and controlling those on the floor.

Minnesota authorities initially believed the gangsters were from Chicago. They cited, among other things, that they were all well versed in their profession and handled the entire situation in such a cool manner, that it's not probable they were amateurs. They were technically right; Keating and Holden had Illinois roots, but now made their home elsewhere. Although it was their first big robbery, they were well trained and had an experienced supporting cast.

Outside of one bandit getting shot, the first bank robbery of the Keating-Holden gang was largely a success. They got away with $42,000 in currency and gold and about $30,000 in negotiable securities.

Keating and Holden were the only official members of their gang and often enlisted the help of other bank robbers and willing accomplices. Although contrary to Bailey's rules, sometimes their ladies would also participate and drive one of the getaway cars. Describing them as freelance bank robbers would be accurate. Not just any "old hat" would do, they wanted experienced robbers by their sides. The St. Paul underworld had helped them become acquainted with World War I machine gunner and former sheriff-elect turned bank robber, Vern Miller, and Fred Barker of the infamous Ma Barker gang. They also still felt obligated to pay back "Machine Gun" Kelly and Frank Nash, for helping them escape.

During the next year Keating and Holden maintained apartments in St. Paul. Frank Nash, who escaped from Leavenworth on October 19, 1930, soon hooked up with them and they helped him lay low. Nash established an apartment in Minnesota under an alias name and was more than willing to participate in his favorite pastime.

Keating and Holden were with each other practically all

Keating-Holden Bank Robberies – Methods of Operation

Method of Operation (M.O.)	Bank of Willmar Minnesota	South Side State Bank Green Bay	Kraft State Bank Menomonie
Date	July 15, 1930	July 20, 1931	October 19, 1931
Day of Week	Tuesday	Monday	Tuesday
Time	10:15 a.m.-10:30 a.m.	11:00 a.m.	9:00 a.m.-9:15a.m.
Small Town	Yes	Yes	Yes
Number of Bandits	7	7	4-6
Weapons	Tommy submachine guns, automatic pistols	Tommy submachine guns, automatic pistols	Tommy submachine guns, automatic pistols
Bandit's Descriptions	Wore suits and hats, "swarthy" (e.g. dark skin, complexion)	Wore suits and hats, "Italian looking".	Wore suits and hats, dark complexion.

Arrival M.O.	Parked in front of bank.	Parked in front of bank.	Parked down from bank, later rolled up to front of it.
Robbery M.O.	One posted outside with Tommy gun, one remained at the door (leader), and three took the cash, gold, and securities.	One remained in vehicle with Tommy gun, another remained at the door (leader), and three took cash, gold, and securities.	One remained outside at the door with Tommy gun, one remained at the door (leader), and three took the cash, gold, and securities.
Escape M.O.	Shot their way out of town.	Shot their way out of town.	Shot their way out of town.
Number of vehicles used	2	2	2
Getaway vehicle driven by female	Yes	Possible. Reported by a witness south of Green Bay.	Unknown
Wore Steel Vests	Unknown	Yes – suspected	Yes – confirmed

of the time. When not out robbing, bootlegging, or engaging in some other illegal venture, they passed their time away playing golf daily at leading public courses. They rode out the winter of 1930 and welcomed in the New Year.

During the summer of 1931, Keating and Holden's gang of regulars now included St. Paul underworld figures Nash, Verne Miller, Charles Harmon, Frank Webber, Jack Snyder, and Harvey Bailey. During this same time period, Keating owned and drove a maroon colored Buick coupe and a maroon colored Buick sedan. A maroon-colored vehicle was seen fleeing the scene of the Green Bay robbery. Was this one of the vehicles owned and driven by Keating?

On July 20, 1931, the very same day of the South Side State Bank Robbery, a long distance phone call was placed from Holden to his wife's (Lillian) relatives in Minoqua, Wis. Was the purpose of this call to confirm the arrival of Holden later that day after the Green Bay robbery?

These and many other similarities of the South Side State Bank Robbery, when compared to the Bank of Willmar and the Kraft State Bank robberies, bear the mark of a Bailey planned and executed bank robbery. Recall that Keating and Holden were not only Bailey trained; they were also well acquainted with him. The method of operation, from the number of vehicles and bandits involved, the methods used inside and outside the bank, weapons carried, the nature of the getaway, and even the physical descriptions of the bandits are similar. The comparison chart on the preceding pages clearly displays these similarities.

What would explain why at least one less bandit participated in the Kraft State Bank robbery? It is possible that the one who had been shot during the South Side State Bank robbery later died from his wounds? Conflicting reports have been received that a body of an unidentified bandit was found near Marinette, Wis., and across the Wisconsin and Minnesota border near St. Paul. Coroner and medical

The former home of Det. August "Gus" Delloye at 1168 E. Walnut St. Delloye spent time there tending his garden and practicing his firearm skills in his basement shooting range. (Photo by Mike R. Knetzger.)

examiner records have been extensively searched and these claims have not been substantiated.

Furthermore, after the South Side State Bank robbery, law enforcement agencies monitored all major intersections leading away from Green Bay in all directions. However, the getaway vehicles were never seen again. Why? Because they probably took rough country roads all the way back to St. Paul, just like they were trained to do.

Keating, Holden, and Bailey's freedom came to an end on July 7, 1932. Playing the game they so loved at the Old Mission Golf Club in Johnson County, Kan., all three of them were apprehended by FBI agents and Kansas City police officers. Keating and Holden were returned to Leavenworth from where they had escaped. Bailey was tried and convicted for a bank robbery that he committed in Fort Scott, Kan., and sentenced to 10 to 50 years at the Kansas State Prison.

Keating and Holden were never held responsible for the Kraft State Bank robbery. Written accounts indicate that the Menomonie authorities were never notified of their apprehension and therefore were never questioned about it. The FBI didn't have jurisdiction over bank robberies at this time and probably didn't question them about it. However, the FBI was aware that Keating and Holden were wanted for the Kraft State Bank robbery. A typewritten account on Keating's criminal history indicates, "As Francis L. Keating, robbed Kraft St. Bank at Menomonie, Wis., on 10-20-31. Warrant issued charging murder, bank robbery and assault with intent to kill. Notify (when apprehended) district attorney, Menomonie, Wis… Notified 7-18-32."

Keating's criminal record clearly indicates that, according to the FBI, they did indeed notify Menomonie authorities of his arrest. Why Keating was never questioned or held accountable is still a mystery. As a result, Green Bay Police were also never notified and never had the chance to interview Keating, Holden, or even Bailey about their potential involvement in the South Side State Bank robbery.

Bailey's autobiography, "Robbing Banks Was My Business: The Story of J. Harvey Bailey, America's Most Successful Bank Robber," doesn't mention the South Side State Bank robbery. He alleged that he was unable to recall the exact locations of the many bank robberies he committed or participated in. It is not known if he was ever questioned about the Green Bay robbery, but as a fellow Wisconsinite, this city was no stranger to him.

Keating went on to serve out his time at Leavenworth and later Alcatraz. He was released from prison in 1948 and returned to Minneapolis where he began an honest living. He owned a flower shop, became a successful organizer for a St. Paul machinist's union, and later remarried. In July of 1978, he died in a nursing home in St. Louis Park, Minn.

Holden chose a different path than his good friend. He

left Alcatraz in 1948 and moved home to Chicago. Soon after, in a drunken rage, he murdered his wife and two of her brothers. He was captured in 1951 and sentenced to 25 years in the Illinois State Penitentiary at Joliet where he died from health related problems two years later.

We will never know, beyond a reasonable doubt, who terrorized the streets of Titletown, U.S.A. on that fateful day in 1931. The physical evidence, suspects, police reports, private detective reports, the police officers, and investigators themselves are all gone. However, the bandits were Bailey-trained and graduates of his program. Significant circumstantial evidence and probable cause exists to place the handcuffs on Keating and Holden.

One surviving eyewitness was interviewed for this story and, citing the length of time since the robbery happened, couldn't say for sure if he saw Keating or Holden at the scene. Upon sharing the strong circumstantial evidence to him he turned his healthy, yet aged face towards me, smirked, nodded his head in agreement and said, "I think you got 'em."

Case closed.

EPILOGUE

The building at the scene of the South Side State Bank robbery, 708-710 S. Broadway, no longer stands today. The bank robbery, coupled with the Depression, sent it into financial disaster. On Nov. 23, 1932, the bank closed its doors for good.

For many years, the building remained standing and played host to several businesses until the early 1970s. It was torn down to make way for the new Mason Street bridge that currently stretches over the Fox River.

Whether it's the first time or the next time you find yourself in the 700 block of South Broadway in Titletown, USA look to the west at the green space before getting onto the Mason Street bridge. Reminisce about the South Side State Bank robbery, when Tommy gun rounds pierced the morning air and empty shell casings littered the streets. Maybe a metal detector could dig up a piece of history…

ABOUT THE AUTHORS

Tracy C. Ertl

Tracy C. Ertl is a former *Green Bay Press-Gazette* police reporter and currently dispatches police officers and firefighters throughout Titletown. Ertl was named 2004 Brown County Telecommunicator of the Year, another high point in her career that started 12 years ago with the Green Bay Police Department. Brown County Public Safety Communications is her employer since Green Bay merged into a joint operation.

As a life-long crime chaser, Ertl began her writing career as a crime reporter and was managing editor of "Lifestyle" magazine in the Fox Valley. She is an award-winning author, most recently taking third place nationwide in the 2005 National Shooting Sports Foundation's writing contest.

Ertl has two books set for release in 2006 including *When the Easter Bunny is Naked,* a non-fiction account of crime survival through the eyes of a child. Also set for release is *Like Riding an Ali-gator,* a personal look at dispatching for the most prominent NFL city in the country, Titletown.

Tracy lives in Green Bay, Wis., with her husband, Terry, and their three teenage children, Andrew, Christine, and Bradley. Christine, 16, a writer as well, is collaborating on a sequel to *When the Easter Bunny is Naked,* titled *Face in the Doorway.*

Mike R. Knetzger

Mike R. Knetzger is a 13-year law enforcement veteran and currently an Advanced Patrol Officer with the city of Green Bay. Prior to policing in Titletown, USA he spent four years as a patrol officer and detective with the Town of Brookfield, Wis., police department.

In additional to several law enforcement certifications, Mr. Knetzger also has an associate degree in police science from Waukesha County Technical College, a bachelor's degree in justice and public policy from Concordia University, and a master's degree in public administration from the University of Wisconsin-Oshkosh. He also teaches criminal justice courses for Northeast Wisconsin Technical College and Colorado Technical University Online.

Knetzger has written several articles on computer crime. This is his first narrative non-fiction book. He lives in Titletown with his wife, Lisa, and their three children.

BIBLIOGRAPHY

"2 Bandits Buried in Potters Field." *The Dunn County News.* 5 Nov 1931.

"2 Policemen Discharged by Chief Hawley." *Green Bay Press-Gazette.* 19 March 1929.

"20 More Shot Removed From Body of Delloye" *Green Bay Press-Gazette.* 14 January 1928.

"Attempt to Siphon Gas From Officer's Auto." *Green Bay Press-Gazette,* 25 July 1931.

Balousek, Marv (1993). *More Wisconsin Crimes of the Century.* Badger Books, Oregon, Wis.

Baye, Bernie. 2005. Interviewed by authors.

"Blackmailers Demand $1000 From Woman." *Green Bay Press-Gazette,* 18 January 1928.

"Blackmailers of Green Bay Man Not Found." *Green Bay Press-Gazette.* 12 January 1928.

Buck, Phillip. 2004. Interviewed by authors.

Caffrey, R. J. FBI Report. 12 July 1932.

Caffrey, R. J. FBI Report. 29 July 1932.

Caffrey, R. J. FBI Report. 1 August 1932.

Cannard, Richard. 2003. Interviewed by authors.

"Chief Hawley Exonerated." *Green Bay Press-Gazette,* 10 April 1929.

"Check Bullets in Effort to Find Bandits." *Green Bay Press-Gazette,* 25 July 1931.

Compton, Harold. 2004-2005. Interviewed by authors.

"Couple Slain in Roadhouse — Victims Found in Bed, Heads Mashed." *Green Bay Press-Gazette,* May 20, 1930.

Delaruelle, Wendell. 2004. Interviewed by authors.

"Desperadoes Visit Willmar." *Willmar Daily Tribune,* 15 July 1930.

"Detective Delloye Wounded." *Green Bay Press-Gazette,* 10 January 1928.

Dunn County Historical Society. *"Kraft State Bank Robbery."* Retrieved February 2, 2005 from www.discover-net. net/dchs/history/exkraft.html.

Dwyer, Clement, W. (1931). Written communication to City of Green Bay, Law Offices of Dwyer & Dwyer, Green Bay, Wis.

"Eau Claire Lakes Area is Searched for Bank Robbers." *Green Bay Press-Gazette,* 24 Oct 1931.

"Fail to Identify Suspect as Bandit." *The Dunn County News,* 5 Nov 1931.

Federal Bureau of Investigation. Criminal Record of Francis L. Keating. 4 September 1934.

Federal Bureau of Investigation. Criminal Record of Thomas Holden. 4 September 1934.

"Fifty Years Can't Bury Double-Hatchet Murder." *Green Bay Press-Gazette,* 14 June 1980.

"Find Burned Car of Bank Bandits Near Cambridge" *The Dunn County News.* 29 Oct 1931.

"Find Second Bandit Dead at Shell Lake." *The Dunn County News.* 22 Oct 1931.

"Five Bandits Make Escape After Forcing the Employees and Customers to Lie on the Floor. Women and Boy on Street are Wounded" *Willmar Daily Tribune,* 15 July 1930.

Glass, J.D. FBI Report. 11 May 1932.

Glass, J.D. FBI Report. 2 June 1932.

Glass, J.D. FBI Report. 10 June 1932.

Glass, J.D. FBI Report. 27 June 1932.

Glass, J.D. FBI Report. 28 June 1932.

"Green Bay Robbery Suspects Released." *Green Bay Press-Gazette,* 22 July 1931.

Green Bay Police Department. History Card of August Delloye. 1916-1965.

Green Bay Police Department. History Card of Thomas

Hawley. 1893-1946.

Haley, J. Evetts (1973). *Robbing Banks Was My Business: The Story of J. Harvey Bailey, America's Most Successful Bank Robber.* Palo Duro Press, Canyon, Texas.

Hardy, S. W. FBI Report. 6 April 1932.

"Hold-Up Gang at Green Bay Gets $12,000." *The Milwaukee Journal,* 20 July 1931.

Holden, Thomas. "High Interest Documents." National Archives and Records Administration, Pacific Region, San Bruno, Calif.

"Inn Murder Case Clue Found?" *Green Bay Press-Gazette,* 30 September 1930.

"James Kraft, 21, Found Dead Beside Shot Thug." *The Dunn County News,* 22 Oct 1931.

Keating, J. J. FBI Report. 24 February 1932.

"Laughs and Thrills Galore In Chase of Bank Robbers." *Green Bay Press-Gazette,* 22 July 1931

Larson, Wm. FBI Report. 3 March 1930

"Little Bohemia," Retrieved November 29, 2004, from Court TV'S Crime Library Web Site: http://www.crimelibrary.com/gangsters_outlaws/outlaws/dillinger/1.html.

"Lt. Delloye Ends Four Decades in Police Dept." *Green Bay Press-Gazette.* 1 May 1956.

Lyman, Michael, D. & Potter, Gary, W. (2004). *Organized Crime (3rd ed.).* Prentice Hall, Upper Saddle River, N.J.

Maccabee, Paul (1995). *"John Dillinger Slept Here — A Crooks' Tour of Crime and Corruption in St. Paul, 1920-1936.* The Minnesota Historical Society Press, St. Paul, Minn.

"Machine Gun Thugs Battle Police; Get Away in Fast Auto." *Green Bay Press-Gazette,* 20 July 1931.

"Menomonie Bank Robbed; 2 Killed." *Green Bay Press-Gazette,* 20 Oct 1931.

"Menomonie Bank Burglars Dodge Trailing Posse." *Green Bay Press-Gazette,* 20 Oct 1931.

Moede, Illa, H. (2003). Written communication.

"Monthly Report Regarding Providing Funds for Police Dept." *Proceedings of the Council of the City of Green Bay.* 21 July 1931.

"No Developments in Bank Robbery Here." *Green Bay Press-Gazette,* 23 July 1931.

"No New Developments in Waupun Blackmail Probe." *Green Bay Press-Gazette,* 19 January 1928.

"Offer $100 Reward For Clues to Blackmailers." *Green Bay Press-Gazette,* 17 January 1928.

"Officers Oran Wall and J. Fenske Made Defendants in Suit." *Green Bay Press-Gazette.* 12 January 1928.

"Police Commission Told Arrest Story About 'Cop' Untrue." *Green Bay Press-Gazette,* 14 January 1928.

"Police, After Blackmailers, Stage Battle — Case of Mistaken Identity Nearly Results Fatally Here. *Green Bay Press-Gazette,* 10 January 1928.

"Police Cars Leave on Hot Robbery Tip." *Green Bay Press-Gazette,* 22 July 1931.

"Policeman Had Right to Leave City; McGillian — Mayor Upholds Officers Who Went After Blackmailer. *Green Bay Press-Gazette,* 11 January 1928.

"Police Silent About Cannard Developments. *Green Bay Press-Gazette.* 11 January 1928.

"Post Rewards for Capture of Bandits." *The Dunn County News,* 22 Oct 1931.

National Archives Regional Office. Prison jacket of Francis L. Keating. San Bruno, Calif.

Ray, David. 2005. Interviewed by authors.

Raymaker, Laverne. 2003-2005. Interviewed by authors.

"Retiring Chief Feted at Dinner." *Green Bay Press-Gazette.* 3 June 1946.

Richetti, Adam, C. *Conspiracy to Deliver a Federal Prisoner.* Retrieved February 2, 2005 from Federal Bureau of Investigation Web Site: http://www.fbi.gov/librief/historic/

famcases/floyd/floyd.html.

"Rites Tuesday For Ex-Chief." *Green Bay Press-Gazette,* 23 March 1951.

"Route Taken by Robbers Now Traced." *Willmar Daily Tribune.* 23 July 1930.

"Sheriff Told Man Admitted Killing People." *Green Bay Press-Gazette,* 30 September 1930.

Slupinski, Julia Dorothy, 2005. Interviewed by the authors.

Smith, D.O. FBI Report. 18 August 1932.

"Somebody Should Introduce These New Policemen" *Green Bay Press-Gazette,* 13 January 1928.

St. Mary's Hospital. *Medical Records of August Delloye.* January 1928.

St. Mary's Hospital. *Medical Records of August Delloye.* July-Aug 1931.

"Teller-tale: Robbery of '31Revisited." *Green Bay Press-Gazette,* 14 July 1985.

"Ten Join in Charges Against Chief Hawley." *Green Bay Press-Gazette,* 18 March 1929.

"The Bank Robber." Retrieved November 29, 2004, from Court TV's Crime Library web site: http://www.crimelibrary. com/gangsters_outlaws/kelly/5.html.

"Think Body of Another Bank Robber Found." *Green Bay Press-Gazette,* 22 Oct 1931.

"Think Menomonie Bandits Robbed South Side State Bank." *Green Bay Press-Gazette,* 22 Oct 1931.

"Two Arrested in S.S. Bank Holdup." *Green Bay Press-Gazette,* 21 July 1931.

"Uncover Inn Murder Clue — Strange Man Seen Leaving Place Monday." *Green Bay Press-Gazette,* 21 May 1930.

Van Beckum, Norb. 2005. Interviewed by authors.

Van Veghel, John and Diane. 2005. Interviewed by authors.

White, T.B. Bureau of Prisons Report. 20 October

1930.

Wisconsin Bankers Association. *Minutes of Mid-Winter Meeting: Executive Council.* 24 Jan 1928.

"Wounded Men Seen in Car Being Sought." *Green Bay Press-Gazette,* 28 July 1931.

Index

Communications 191
Buchanan, Dr. R.C. 80
Buck, Phillip 114, 117
Burdon's Hill 133
Burke, Martin 19, 41, 82, 94,
    100, 109, 116, 124,
    128, 129, 130, 136-
    139, 140, 151, 152,
    165, 174

A

Ahearn, O.W. 141
Al's Hamburgers 170
Alcatraz 188
Allen, Norbert 105
American Bankers Associa-
    tion 140, 141
Antigo, Wis. 85
Appleton, Wis. 151, 152
Appleton Police Department
    135
Arndt, Raymond 114
Associated Press 174

B

Bailey, J. Harvey 179, 180,
    186-189
Bank of Willmar 182, 186
Barker, Fred 183
Barker, Ma 183
Barnes, George "Machine
    Gun Kelly" 7, 178,
    181
Bay West Paper Company 15
Belleau's Drug Store 98
Birdsall, Lucille 5, 37, 59,
    89, 94, 95
Blecha, Michael 5
Bodart, Eddie 64
Brown County, Wis. 134,
    191
Brown County Jail 83
Brown County Library 6
Brown County Public Safety

C

Cambridge, Wis. 164
Cannard, Arthur 19, 46
Cannard, Anice 22, 25, 46,
    51
Cannard, Marie 15
Cannard, Richard 22, 25,
    46, 51
Cannard, William H. 13
Capone, Al 7, 140, 176
Carney, Bill 135, 138
Cayer, Earl 105, 124, 130,
    139, 140, 150
Chapter, Howard 174
Chicago, Ill. 7, 102, 149,
    151, 153, 177, 179,
    183, 188
City Stadium 13
Cleveland, Ohio 166
Clifford, Dr. 114
Clowry, Irene 94
Coleman, Undersheriff 140
Colorado Technical Univer-
    sity Online 192
Concordia University 192
Coy, Bernard 89, 93
Cronce, Otto 49, 82, 125

D

DaNamur 109
DeBroux, Mrs. William 64,
   72
DeBroux, Martin 73
DeCock, Dr. 34
DeGroot, Al 129
DeGroot & Allen 129
Delaney, Simon 27
Delaruelle, Lloyd 115
Delloye, August "Gus" 5, 18,
   38, 55, 100, 109, 119,
   129, 142, 143, 147,
   149, 153, 156, 158,
   165, 168, 169, 171,
   173
Delloye, Mrs. 36, 117, 131,
   145, 148
DeNamur, Elmer 103, 109,
   119, 174
De Voursney, A.M. 140
Diener, John V. 142
Dillinger, John 7, 105, 134,
   140, 175
Donnelly, Thomas 92, 94
Don Quixote Supper Club 87
Dwyer, Clement W. 142, 157

E

East High School 13
Ertl, Tracy C. 191

F

Faikel, Clem 114
Farmer's Exchange Bank 56
FBI 140, 166, 177, 179, 187,
   188

Feikel, Officer 124
Foss, W. G. 89
Fox River 190
Frawley, John 151
Frechette, Evelyn 105, 175

G

Garhusky, Frank 129
Geo Buck's Grocery Store
   98
Geyer, James 28, 34
Gilmore and Erdmann's Bar-
   bershops 98
Golden, William 105, 150
Golden Pheasant Roadhouse
   8, 60, 61, 71, 80, 91,
   102
Gosin, P.J. 80
Grayson, Frances W. 14
Grebel, V.E. 41
Grebel-Jossart Electric Com-
   pany 41
Greenleaf, Wis. 174
Green Bay Packers 13
Green Bay Press-Gazette 5,
   8, 52, 53, 58, 63, 85,
   89, 135, 137, 149,
   165, 166, 168, 175,
   191

H

Harmon, Charles Preston
   164, 186
Hawley, Chief Thomas E. 5,
   38, 47, 56, 99, 109,
   113, 131, 142, 166
Hodek, Frank 81
Holden, Thomas "Tommy"

165, 174, 177, 179,
183, 186-189
Holden, Lillian 179, 186
Hoover, J. Edgar 166
Huth, Mrs. Henry 128

I

Illinois, state of 62, 183
Illinois State Penitentiary
189
Indiana, state of 175
Iowa City, Iowa 150

J

Johnson County, Kan. 187
Joliet, Ill. 189
Juster, A.W. 109

K

Kansas City, Mo. 174, 187
Keating, Francis L. 165, 174,
177, 179, 182, 183,
186, 188, 189
Kelly, Dr. 42
Kelly, "Machine Gun" *(see
George "Machine
Gun Kelly" Barnes)*
Kelly Lake 14
Kenosha County, Wis. 179
Kerin, Lois 175
Knetzger, Michael R. 192
Kraft, James 161
Kraft, William 164
Kraft State Bank 160, 186,
188
Kupsack *(Lucille's ex-hus-
band)* 83

L

Lament, "Fish Eye" 172
Leavenworth prison 164,
174, 187
Lee, Peter 87
Lee, Phillip 87
Lee's Cantonese restaurant
86
Lehey, Mr. 138
Lewellen, District Attorney
83
Libgott, John 135, 138
Little Bohemia 175

M

Malchow, Mrs. 127
Manitowish Waters, Wis.
175
Marinette, Wis. 186
Matthews, Fred 78
Mayo Clinic 131, 143
McDermott, J.B. 115, 116
McGillion, Mayor 39
Meert, Frank 149
Menomonie, Wis. 160, 164,
165, 188
Michigan, state of 150
Military Order of the Purple
Heart 174
Miller, Geraldine 124, 126
Miller, Verne 181, 183
Milwaukee, Wis. 62, 80, 94,
153
Minnesota. state of 134, 164,
182, 183, 186
Minnesota Bureau of Crimi-
nal Apprehension 165
Minocqua, Wis. 179

Mississippi River 134
Morgan, Frank 139
Muraski, Jeremy 6

N

Nash, Frank 183
Nelson, George "Baby Face" 7
New Holstein, Wis. 153
Nickolai, Sheriff 82, 83, 93, 94
Noel, Thelis 56
Northeast Wisconsin Technical College 192

O

O'Connor, Harry T. 166
O'Shea, Raphael E. 98
Ohio, state of 175
Old Mission Golf Club 187

P

Pankratz Motor Car Co. 129
Patton, Sgt. 109, 124, 125, 128, 130, 133
Prim, Chief 135, 138

R

Racine, Wis. 172
Ray, David 87
Red Blacks Tavern 175
Rommelyer, R. A. 160
Roosevelt, President Franklin 103

S

Sager, Bernice "Bea" 104, 124, 126
Saltis, Joe 7, 140, 176
Senn, Dr. 131, 146, 154, 155
Seering, Dr. George 143, 145-147
Shawano, Wis. 140
Shawano County Sheriff's Department 133
Sheboygan, Wis. 91, 93
Sheboygan County Jail 92
Shenandoah, Iowa 179
Shorty' Van Pee's Soda Parlor 26
Silvermen, Sammy 181
Slupinski, Frank 5, 104, 124, 130, 139, 140, 150
Slupinski, Jean 107
Slupinski, Julia Dorothy (Altman) 5, 107
Smits, Bea 175
Snyder, Jack 186
South Dakota, state of 175
South Side Clothing Company 98
St. Louis Park, Minn. 188
St. Mary's Hospital 32, 136
St. Paul, Minn. 7, 97, 135, 160, 164, 179, 183, 186
St. Willebrord's 60, 86
Sturgeon Bay, Wis. 69, 91

T

Taylor, John 139
Tickler's Hardware Store 98
Townsend, Vernon 161
Town of Brookfield, Wis. 192
Town of Preble, Wis. 26, 65

Triangle Club 15, 17, 25, 27,
    30, 42, 45, 53, 56
Tucson Police Dept. 175

U

University of Wisconsin 6
University of Wisconsin
    – Oshkosh 192

V

Vandenboom, Mrs. George
    129
Van Beckum, Norb Van 60,
    79, 86
Van Vondern, E.J. 129
Van Veghel, John "Jack" 5,
    59, 62, 85, 95
Van Veghel, Peter 82, 86
Verheygen, Martin 64
Volstead Act - Prohibition 99

W

Wall, Oran 26
Walters, William 26, 38
Waukesha County Technical
    College 192
Waupun, Wis. 53
Webber, Frank 163, 186
Webb Lake, Wis. 164
WHBY, radio 137
Wisconsin Bankers Associa-
    tion 140